KU-204-433

The New Inflation:
The Politics of Prices
and Incomes

50 0072014 1

TELEPEN

Students and External Readers	Staff & Research Students
DATE DUE FOR RETURN	**DATE OF ISSUE**
10.OCT 79 0 0 9	
19.MAR 82 0 3 0	
16.MAR 83 0 0 3 2	
 UNIVERSITY LIBRARY THIS ITEM RETURN ON	
	N.B. All books must be returned for the Annual Inspection in June

Any book which you borrow remains your responsibility until the loan slip is cancelled

3

AUBREY JONES

The New Inflation:
The Politics of Prices and Incomes

ANDRE DEUTSCH

First published 1973 by
André Deutsch Limited
105 Great Russell Street London WC1

Copyright © 1973 by Aubrey Jones
All rights reserved

Printed in Great Britain by
Fletcher & Son Ltd, Norwich

ISBN 0 233 96443 6

Published by arrangement with Penguin Books Limited

Contents

Acknowledgements

Many minds have shaped mine in the writing of this book, but I should express especial thanks to Dudley Jackson of St Catharine's College, Cambridge; to Professor H. A. Turner of Churchill College, Cambridge; to Dr Allan Fels, formerly of the Department of Applied Economics, Cambridge; and to Mr Bob Hepple of Clare College, Cambridge. A generous grant from the Nuffield Foundation made possible the valuable assistance of research staff of the Department of Applied Economics as well as its typing, computing and library staff, and also made it easier for me to spend time in Cambridge working on the book. I am much indebted to the Master and Fellows of Churchill College for electing me an Honorary Industrial Fellow Commoner and for their cordial hospitality. The History Faculty kindly provided me with a room in their magnificent new building.

This book is dedicated to all those who shared with me the pioneering effort of the Prices and Incomes Board.

Aubrey Jones
8 January 1973

Introduction

In December 1964 Mr (now Lord) George Brown, then the United Kingdom's First Secretary of State and Secretary of State for Economic Affairs in a newly elected Labour Government, succeeded in securing the agreement of the representative organizations of employers and trade unions to sign with the Government a Statement of Intent – the employers not to raise prices too much, the union leaders not to push wages too high, both to press harder for efficiency, and the Government to promote growth and so increase real standards of living. A National Board for Prices and Incomes was to be established to help the parties keep to their intentions.

Towards the end of February 1965 Mr Brown was composing his Board. Unexpectedly, I, a Conservative Member of Parliament and therefore a member of the Parliamentary Opposition, was invited to become the Board's Chairman. After some ten days of careful thought I accepted, but the decision was not an easy one.

The case against can be easily stated. There had been similar bodies other than the proposed Prices and Incomes Board (as it subsequently became known in newspapers): the Council on Prices, Productivity and Incomes (colloquially known as 'The Three Wise Men'), which published four reports between its formation in 1957 and its unannounced demise in 1961; and the National Incomes Commission, which published four reports and one interim report between 1962 and 1965. The first had passed into history, the second was about to go. And eminent names had tangled themselves with failure. This was a frightening thought, emphasized by the cry of 'impracticability' one met everywhere. And the sense of fright was to endure, long after the

debate within my own mind was ended. Then there was the fact of
enforced departure from the House of Commons, for the new
Chairmanship was an office of profit under the Crown and thus
incompatible with continued Membership of the House. Few
contemplate lightly departure from the House of Commons;
and without cogent reasons I would not have been one of
them.

The case for acceptance was, on the other hand, strong. I had
been a Minister; but what was a Minister? The occupant for a
couple of years of a Department of State, numerous in its layers
of staff, tenacious in its traditions, and massive to move. One
scarcely in fact moved it. An apparent shift could be made on the
surface for an odd year or so, but the changes were soon shrugged
off and the Department reverted to its ways. The new Chairmanship at least offered a reasonable length of time – five years;
and a chance to do something more fundamental than a Departmental Minister could do. But could more fundamental
policies be carried out? The bodies mentioned in the preceding
paragraph all represented attempts by Governments of both
the main political parties in the United Kingdom to introduce a
so-called prices and incomes policy. What lay behind this
persistence? Was it the deference of Ministers of more than one
party to Government officials whose thinking ran in one revolving
groove? Or was it rather the inevitable response of men in
authority to new post-war economic and political issues; a
groping for solutions to problems which had not previously
existed? Was it the case that this was the way in which history
moved, the tide advancing a little, retreating somewhat less,
advancing, retreating, but finally rushing inexorably in? There
was at any rate a chance that the last was the true explanation of
the recurrent emphasis on prices and incomes.

The post I was being asked to take up was a non-party one.
And acceptance of it as such was endorsed by an official committee of the Conservative party. But suppose it had not been,
what then? Are all politics in a two-party political system bound
to be sharply divided between Government and Opposition?
Is there no room for some role of reconciliation across the
divide, some expression of a wider unity which the parties have

now forgotten? These arguments and questions decided me in favour of accepting.

The point of writing about my time at the Prices and Incomes Board, several years after the event, is not to chronicle subsequent happenings, except incidentally. My purpose is to gauge what was done right and what was done wrong; and, in the light of this experience, to draw the lessons which seem to me appropriate and essential both for Great Britain's future and for that of other countries grappling with the same complex of problems.

That complex of problems revolves around the word 'inflation', for the cure of which many diverse remedies are propounded. The purpose of the book is to advance an explanation of the phenomenon as seen in contemporary political and economic terms; to consider whether or not the more conventional and mainly economic remedies are adequate; to study the application of the newer and more overtly political remedy of a prices and incomes policy; to rebut the critics of such a policy on both the Left and the Right of the political spectrum; and finally to point the way forward. This is not a detailed study of the working of the Prices and Incomes Board. That subject has been adequately covered in descriptive studies by Dr Allan Fels in *The British Prices and Incomes Board** and by Dr Joan Mitchell in *The National Board for Prices and Incomes*;† the present book is concerned to provide a political and economic *analysis* of the problem of inflation in contemporary industrialized societies.

* Cambridge University Press, 1972.
† Secker & Warburg, 1972.

Part 1

Why Have a Prices and Incomes Policy?

Chapter One

Why Inflation Matters

Inflation is the key post-war economic problem, just as unemployment was the key economic problem of the inter-war
world. By and large inflation has shown itself in a relentless,
though at most times moderate, rise in some index of prices. The
rate of increase may vary between 3 and 6 or more per cent a year,
though at the beginning of the '70s the rate appeared to be
accelerating and in the United Kingdom was approaching double
figures. Like the inter-war problem of unemployment, inflation
is also an international problem. It obtains in nearly all industrialized countries; it obtains in countries in the process of
industrializing themselves; it obtains particularly in smaller
countries adjacent to larger countries, such as the Irish Republic
in relation to the United Kingdom or Canada in relation to the
United States; and it probably obtains in Communist countries,
though its manifestation there may be more concealed.

Continuous, though moderate, inflation persisting for a gener-
ation is a new phenomenon, earlier history having been punc-
tuated by short, steep increases in prices followed by decreases.
The increases might take place during wars and the decreases
might alternate around a slowly rising or slowly declining trend.
The universality of the problem is also new, and may be due to
the growth in international trade and thus to the transmission of
inflation through trade from one country to another. Equally it
may be due to the fact that countries may be undergoing roughly
the same kind of social evolution, born of roughly similar
political ideals.

Various measures of the movement in prices may be taken.
First there are prices to the consumer. Their movement may be
measured over time by the 'price' or total cost of a basket of

goods and services representing the mix of purchases of an 'average' consumer. This measure is known in the United Kingdom as the Retail Price Index. Alternatively the composition of the basket may be changed more frequently to reflect more accurately the changing patterns of consumption, the resulting measure being known as a cost of living index. There is, however, no great short-run difference between them. Prices to the consumer in the United Kingdom – their course over this century is shown in Chart 1 – have moved faster than in most other Western European countries.

Another picture of inflation is given by the movement of an index of export prices. This is a crude measure, in that it is obtained by dividing the total value of exports by a volume index; strictly speaking, it is therefore the 'unit value' of exports. This is an important pointer to international competitiveness, reflecting the ability of a country to export, or to withstand a flood of imports, in so far as changes in exports and imports are determined by price changes. By this measure also inflation has moved faster in the United Kingdom than in most other major industrialized countries.

A different, but more relevant, measure is the movement in the price of the gross domestic product (GDP) – that is, of the total output, or value added, in a country of both goods and services.* This price is derived in the United Kingdom by taking the ratio between the money value of the gross domestic product

* Gross Domestic Product (GDP)	Total output of a given economy in a given period. It is thus the *maximum* that could be devoted to consumption, given that worn-out capital is not replaced.
Net Domestic Product	GDP less the amount of capital goods (machinery, equipment, etc.) necessary to replace the amount of capital used up in producing the year's GDP. It is thus the maximum output that could be devoted to consumption in a closed economy, while keeping the capital stock intact.
Gross National Product (GNP)	GDP plus net income derived from the ownership of property abroad.
National Income	Net National Product, that is the GNP less the amount required to maintain the capital stock both at home and abroad.

Chart 1 Retail price index, 1900–1970. 1963=100

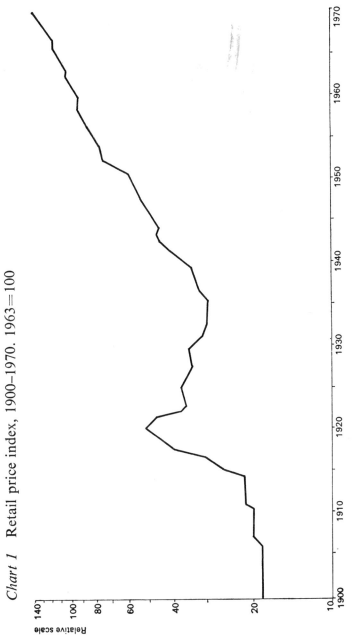

Relative scale

140 — 100 — 80 — 60 — 40 — 20 — 10

1900   1910   1920   1930   1940   1950   1960   1970

Source: London and Cambridge Economic Service, *The British Economy: Key Statistics 1900–1970*, Table E.

and the value as it would have been had prices remained as they were in 1963; it measures therefore the change in 'the price' of a unit of 'real' GDP. Since this measure encompasses exports, investment goods and consumer goods, it is the best overall indicator of a country's performance. And like the export price index this measure has over the last decade or so moved faster in the United Kingdom than in most other major industrial countries.

Apart, however, from its usefulness as a pointer to international competitiveness, the use of a price measure related to the whole of the gross domestic product serves to show how prices are built up, how they are related to incomes and profits, how they are affected by changes in these, and indeed how the product comes to be divided between labour and capital. Since the gross domestic product represents the total output of a country, its money value, when distributed as incomes, is equal to the sum of all wages (including salaries) and all profits (the latter being the residual surplus or difference between the total and wages). Assuming the total output to be unchanged in volume and if profits are to remain unchanged, then the price of the gross domestic product must rise if wages rise. Alternatively, again on the assumption of unchanged output but this time if wages are to remain unchanged, then the price of the gross domestic product will rise if profits rise.

The volume of output need not, of course, remain unchanged; it ought indeed to increase. The amount of labour and the amount of capital can also change. Matters become a little more complicated the moment one takes all these changes into account. The changing volume of output or of the gross domestic product can be related to the changing amount of labour or of capital. If output is increasing but the amount of labour remains the same, we can say that the productivity of labour, or output per employee, is rising. This does not necessarily mean that men are exerting more effort; the increased output may be due to new machines; it means only that output is rising in relation to the amount of labour. Similarly the volume of output can increase in relation to the amount of capital; in that case we can say that the productivity of capital or output per unit of capital is rising.

Again this does not necessarily mean that the increased output is due to capital; it could be due to labour. In practice, however, the main 'contributor' to an increase in output or in the gross domestic product is capital or capital goods – that is to say, machines – and the changing technology which these capital goods represent. The two expressions, the productivity of labour and the productivity of capital, are thus very pertinent to the problem of prices.

Despite the slight complications which we have just introduced the money value of the gross domestic product is still the sum of all wages (including salaries) and profits. Now if wages rise faster than the productivity of labour as just defined – or if, to use a more technical expression, labour costs per unit of output rise – and the rate of profit or return on the capital invested in machines is unchanged, prices will rise. Correspondingly, if the return on capital rises faster than the productivity of capital, again as defined, and wages remain unchanged, prices will rise on this account. Profits, however, are a surplus or a residual; they are not a cost; they are what is left of revenue or receipts after costs. The crucial relationship therefore is that between labour costs per unit of output, on the one hand, and prices, on the other. If labour costs per unit of output rise and prices rise correspondingly, the rate of return on capital or the rate of profit will stay the same. If, on the other hand, prices lag behind the movement in labour costs per unit of output, the rate of profit will be reduced. If, finally, prices run ahead of the increase in labour costs per unit of output, the rate of profit will rise. (For those who like mathematical proof of these propositions, the relevant algebraic equations are set out in the Appendix).

Which measure one chooses as a measure of inflation, whether it be the movement of prices to the consumer, of export prices, or of the price of the gross domestic product, depends on the purpose in hand. When in this book I talk of inflation, and therefore of prices in general as distinct from the prices of individual things, I shall mean the price of the gross domestic product because of its comprehensiveness – it covers prices to the consumer, export prices, the return on capital or profit, and labour costs per unit of output. Important aspects of the increase in the price of the gross domestic product are the increase in labour costs per unit of output and the implication of this latter increase for the rate of profit on capital.

Now why should inflation cause concern? Why should there be a need to do anything about it? The simple answer is that it makes inequalities worse, both of income and of wealth, and is especially harmful to the poorer sections of the community. There are those who argue that if everyone correctly anticipated the rate of inflation the economy would function very much as it would if prices were generally stable. According to the Summary Report of the Canadian Prices and Incomes Commission: 'it should make no difference to . . . actual economic behaviour whether the value of money was declining by X per cent a year or twice X per cent a year. Over time, the prices at which all economic transactions were conducted would simply be adjusted upward at the appropriate rate'.* The abstract argument may be sound, but societies are politically concerned with modifying the distribution of income and wealth. To say that economic behaviour could continue as before with a correctly anticipated rate of inflation simply evades this important question.

The political concern can indeed be aggravated by inflation. It is difficult to believe that everyone could correctly anticipate the rate of inflation and act with equal facility on the anticipation. In countries such as the United Kingdom and the United States there are a few owners of large blocks of capital and a much larger number of owners of smaller blocks of capital. The owners of the larger blocks can afford to invest more speculatively and are more likely to have the knowledge to do so; they are better able, that is to say, to invest in those sectors likely most quickly to benefit from a rising inflation and to retain their appreciated wealth should the rate of inflation subsequently steady itself. The owners of the smaller blocks of capital, on the other hand, will invest more safely – say, in stocks with a fixed rate of interest, the real value of which will decline as the inflation proceeds. In time, no doubt, the owners of small amounts of wealth will change their habits; but it is doubtful whether

* Prices and Incomes Commission, *Inflation, Unemployment and Incomes Policy*, Ottawa, 1972, p. 30.

they will catch up with the larger capitalists; and at the end of the day the disparity in capital ownership is likely to be increased. Similarly there are a small number of workers with high incomes and a larger number of workers with lower incomes. Even if it be assumed that both sets of workers can correctly anticipate the rate of inflation, the former are usually in a better position than the latter to protect themselves; for they can better afford to move and shop around and they may be better organized, whereas the less well-paid workers are more tied to their localities; they have to accept whatever offers of employment they may have, and they do not have the same wide range of choice in consumption. The discrepancy in real income may therefore be increased, the more so, the faster is the rate of inflation. Furthermore, inflation has very disrupting social effects, particularly in the area of industrial relations. In the post-war period up to 1967, the average number of working days lost through strikes was about 3 million a year. But in 1968 working days lost through industrial stoppages rose to 4·7 million, then to 6·9 million in 1969, to 11 million in 1970, to 13·6 million in 1971, and to 23·9 million for 1972. The continuation of this trend is not something which Britain could afford to ignore.

Inflation can proceed at different rates in different countries. The country in which inflation proceeds the fastest will tend to export less and import more. In the 1950s and 1960s, when, in accordance with the Bretton Woods Agreement of 1945, countries were still trying to keep unchanged the exchange value of their currencies in relation to other currencies, the tendency to import more and export less led in the United Kingdom to a succession of balance of payments crises, each one worse than its predecessor. In 1955 the deficit on the United Kingdom's current account transactions with other countries was £155m.; in 1960 it was £265m.; in 1964 it was £395m.; and in 1967, when the pound was devalued, it was £312m. The means adopted to redress the adverse payments balance was to slow down the rate of economic growth or, in headline terms, to 'squeeze' the economy, so that both consumers and manufacturers bought less from abroad. The slower economic growth brought with it an increase in unemploy-

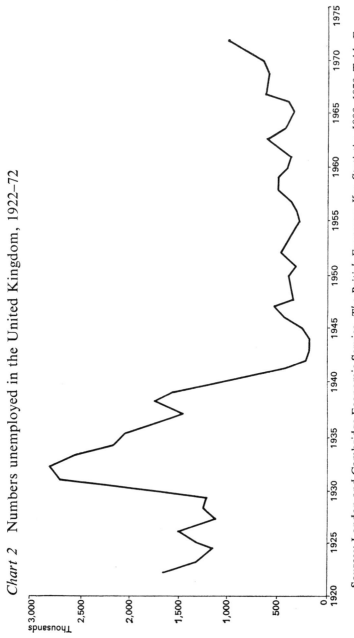

Chart 2   Numbers unemployed in the United Kingdom, 1922–72

Sources: London and Cambridge Economic Service, *The British Economy: Key Statistics 1900–1970*, Table E, and Central Statistical Office, *Monthly Digest of Statistics* (October 1972) Table 21; 1972 is the average of the first three quarters.

ment as is shown in Chart 2. Just as each crisis showed an increased deficit, so each application of the remedy increased unemployment and made it more persistent. In 1959, two years after the squeeze of 1957, the number of wholly unemployed was 512,000; in 1963, two years after the squeeze of 1961, it was 612,000; in 1968, two years after the squeeze of 1966, it was 601,000. Unemployment remained around this mark for the three consecutive years 1967, 1968 and 1969, finally climbing in January 1972 to just over one million. The loss to the community and the pain to individuals implied in the waste of human skill and talent on this scale are disproportionately high; they cannot and should not be neglected.

In the early 1970s governments seemed more willing to allow the rate of exchange with other currencies to fall freely. Rather than incur an overt devaluation from a fixed parity resulting from persistently unfavourable balance of payments, they appeared to be readier to let the rate drop in a free foreign exchange market. This is what the United States Administration did in 1971 and the United Kingdom Government in 1972. The falling rate of exchange may make the future rate of inflation more unpredictable and possibly even worsen it; but more of that later. Suffice it at this juncture to say that the falling rate of exchange, as against a balance of payments crisis, is an alternative way of reflecting the fact that inflation in the country in question has been faster than elsewhere; it does not remove the cause. Governments are still likely to try and remove the cause in the same way as they did when trying to maintain a fixed rate of exchange – by calling a halt to economic growth. The faster the rate of inflation, the more drastic will be the attempt to call a halt.

It is true that the concept of economic growth has now to be tempered by a greater regard for the effect of growth on the environment. Economic growth remains none the less the main vehicle for removing poverty; for extending to the masses those refinements of life, such as education and medical care, which have historically been reserved for the few; and for helping the development of the Third World. Without economic growth the reduction of inequalities both within countries and between countries is much more difficult. Economic growth is, however, threatened by inflation, and attempts to deal with inflation still leave an important residue of unemployment. Until economic growth can be reconciled with a more moderate rate of inflation, the boast that 'capitalism works' remains an empty one. That is why inflation has to be coped with as an important problem comparable to the inter-war problem of unemployment. There can be no coping with it until there is some understanding as to how persistent inflation has come about, and this will be the theme of the next chapter.

It will be the tenor of that chapter that there is now a 'new inflation', resulting from the response of contemporary social forces to economic growth, in contrast to past inflations, which were due to sporadic, temporary and essentially economic influences. This 'new inflation' started on the morrow of the Second World War and has persisted. What is also 'new' about the new inflation is the increased public awareness of, and alarm over, the problem of persistently rising prices caused by the recent acceleration of inflation:

United Kingdom: per cent increase in retail prices over the previous year

1967	1968	1969	1970	1971	1972
2·5	4·7	5·4	6·4	9·4	7·1

The public reaction to this acceleration explains many of the social problems currently confronting Britain, and these problems cannot by themselves be 'solved' without tackling the root causes of the new inflation; which implies that new policies to contain inflation must be expected to form a permanent part of Britain's future economic policies. What, then, are these causes?

Chapter Two

The Causes of the
New Inflation

It used to be accepted that, over the decades for which statistics were available, wages had remained a fairly constant proportion of the national income despite the aim of trade unions to increase wages at the expense of profits. A definitive statement of facts has now been produced by Dr Charles Feinstein of Cambridge University, which suggests a substantial modification of the earlier view.* His figures, represented in Charts 3A and 3B, show that the proportion of the national income going to wages and salaries has increased, particularly since the Second World War; correspondingly the proportion of the national income going to property and to capital has declined. This decline in the proportionate share of capital would have been consistent with a constant rate of profit had the productivity of capital, or output per unit of capital, been rising fast enough to offset it. In fact, the rate of return before tax on capital employed has also declined somewhat, as shown in Chart 4.

The share of wages and salaries in the national income will be determined by the relative movement of unit labour costs and of the general price index; labour costs have moved in advance of prices, thereby raising the share of labour in the national income. The crucial questions are, therefore: why have wage and salary costs per unit of output increased, and why has the price index lagged behind? It will be the theme of this chapter that the conventional theories do not give an adequate explanation and

* C. H. Feinstein, *National Income, Expenditure and Output of the United Kingdom 1855–1965*, Cambridge University Press, 1972, Table 18, p. 144. Dr Feinstein's data were supplemented for the later years from the Central Statistical Office, *National Income and Expenditure 1972*, H M S O, 1972.

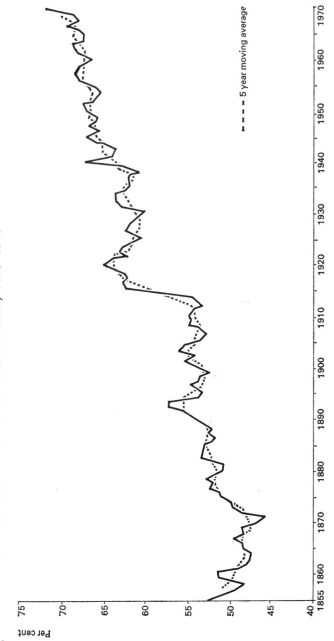

Chart 3A Labour's share in national income, 1855–1969

■ ■ ■ ■ 5 year moving average

Per cent

Chart 3B Labour's share in national income, 1948–69

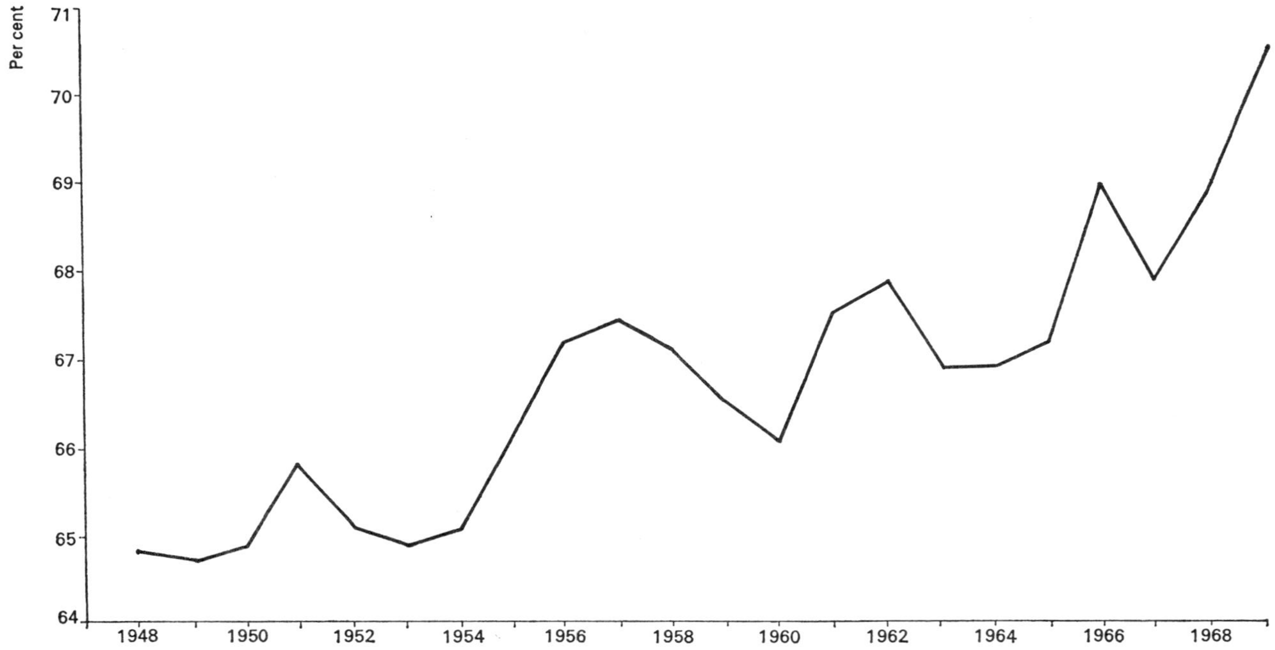

that they make the mistake in particular of seeking only an economic explanation instead of an economic-cum-political one. (To avoid misunderstanding it should be made clear that whenever the word 'wages' is used, it is intended as a shorthand expression to cover both wages and salaries.)

The entire corpus of economic literature from the late eighteenth century up to the Second World War scarcely touched on the problem of wages growing faster than the gross domestic product. The earlier writers treated labour much as they would a commodity. They painted a picture of a mass of undifferentiated workers descending upon an imaginary market place and confronting numerous employers. From the haggling between the two there emerged a wage, a wage which no one member of either side was able to affect, so insignificant was the individual in relation to the total. Little was said of the psychology with which wage and salary-earners entered on this imaginary haggling. To the writers of the early nineteenth century the worker sought a subsistence wage depending 'on the quantity of food, necessaries, and conveniences which become essential to him from habit'.* If wages rose much above this, the population would grow and the very growth in population and therefore in the labour force would tend to keep wages at the subsistence level. This theory was later expanded by Marx who argued that wages would be kept at the subsistence level with the 'surplus value' (or residual profit as we have defined it) created by labour being accumulated by the capitalists and invested in increasing productive capacity. Because of the increasing concentration of income, the productive capacity so created would not be fully utilized, and this, together with rising productivity, would create unemployment and so put a further limit upon wages.

To the writers of the later nineteenth century, wages were determined in very much the same way, but the psychology with which workers and employers entered the market place was somewhat more refined. Workers were described as mentally balancing the disagreeableness of so much extra work against the deprivation of an equivalent amount of leisure. The employer,

* David Ricardo, *On the Principles of Political Economy and Taxation*, John Murray, London 1821, p. 86.

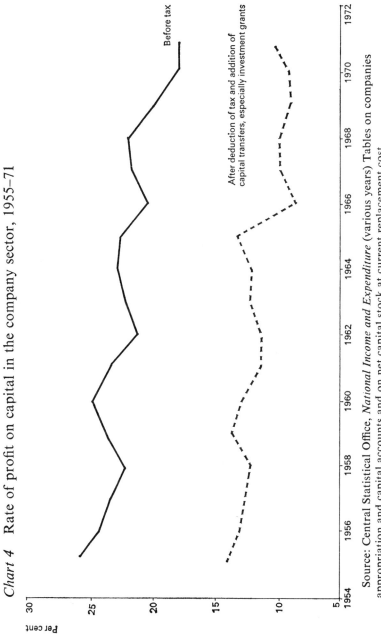

Chart 4 Rate of profit on capital in the company sector, 1955–71

Source: Central Statistical Office, *National Income and Expenditure* (various years) Tables on companies appropriation and capital accounts and on net capital stock at current replacement cost.

for his part, calculated the worth to him of an extra worker (the so-called marginal product) as against the wage determined in the market place, a wage which he was again powerless to affect. After the point of equality between the wage and the marginal worker's contribution to output workers would not be employed. The determination of wages depicted in this way was a very small-scale process, but what was true of an individual employer was also true of all employers together, and so there could be no question of the general wage level increasing faster than the increase in the gross domestic product, for wages would be seen by each and every employer as exceeding the marginal product and there would be unemployment, so acting as a limit to the increase in wages.

The development of trade unionism was then dragged in as an afterthought. Just as a monopolist could corner a commodity and thus affect a 'competitive' market, so a trade union could become a 'monopolist'. But the parallel was not quite complete, for the exercise of a monopoly can carry with it heavier consequences for a trade union than it can for a monopolist in a product. The monopolist in a commodity market could exact from the consumer a price higher than would otherwise prevail by restricting the supply and by accepting the fact that the total volume of sales would be lower than otherwise. The monopolistic trade union might similarly restrict entry into a trade in order to maintain wages, but this restriction of supply would mean unemployment, something scarcely consistent with the brotherhood spirit of a trade union. There was also a natural barrier to the movement of wages from the side of the employers – they would not pay more than the marginal product or the contribution of the additional worker. Any attempt by a trade union to push beyond this point brought its retribution in the shape of unemployment. Again this is a consequence which a trade union would not lightly accept if it were aware that this could indeed be the result of its actions. It is fair to say that Adam Smith in his *Wealth of Nations* thought that there was a natural tendency on the part of employers to conspire together to keep wages down and that defensive collusion by trade unionists was therefore justifiable. The thought, however, was not developed and the stigma attached to a monopoly continues to be attached by some to a trade union.

A departure from the very strong tradition of thinking of these 'limits' on the movement of wages was effected by Keynes on the eve of the Second World War. The nineteenth-century writers, with the exception of Marx, had assumed full employment. Keynes, on the other hand, was preoccupied with the persistence of widespread unemployment. With rising employment, physical resources, including labour, would be drawn into fuller use. When all were fully employed, but not until then, money wages could rise faster than total output. But this thought that wages might rise faster than total output was related to the concept of 'full' employment, something which had previously been assumed but which, it was now accepted, had to be deliberately contrived. Some writers already saw that in that case 'full' employment might need to be accompanied by measures to influence the course of wages. The thought, however, that wages might rise faster than total output even when employment was less than 'full' was still unborn.

An inherited body of thought retains a powerful hold over the minds of men long after the moment of utterance, and the thinking briefly summarized above still does. It is, however, at odds with what we observe in contemporary society, because it would be more realistic to say that the present-day phenomenon is one of 'wage leadership'. In other words a 'leading' sector grants wage increases which set the pace for other sectors to follow. Let us suppose that this leading sector is the one in which the growth in productivity is fastest; then if similar wage increases follow in the sectors in which productivity is growing more slowly, wages in these will be rising faster than productivity, and prices will accordingly need to be raised if the rate of profit is to remain unchanged. Thus the leading sector could be an important force in the inflationary process, particularly if it is a fast-growing sector. Economic growth itself could in that case generate inflation, and one of the key facts of the post-war industrialized world has been, by historical standards, its extremely rapid rate of growth.

A recent study of the Swedish economy concluded that the initiating impulse for wage increases in that country came from the export industries.* These industries had 'room' to pay high wage increases, mostly because the growth of output per man-hour was fast, but partly because the prices of exported products were rising abroad. The rapid wage increases thus initiated were then transmitted to the more 'sheltered' industries with a slower rate of growth in productivity, which then raised their prices, being able to do so because they were not so much under the threat of international competition. The 'transmission' of wage increases occurred because *social* forces in Sweden would not tolerate a slower rate of improvement in living standards for workers employed in the lagging sectors of the economy.

A subsequent and far more widely ranging study concluded that international comparative data did indeed indicate a pattern in which wages rose in line with output per head in the fastest growing industries.† Within any country the more closely other industries' wages followed the leading sector, the greater the pressure on the lagging sectors to raise prices and the higher the country's rate of price inflation. Thus 'the general pace not only of real wage improvement but also of money wage increase will vary with the average rate of productivity growth – *though money wages will always rise faster than productivity*' (my italics).

For present purposes, the important point of this study is that it demonstrates how, on average, wages could rise faster than productivity, that is, why there is a tendency for labour costs per unit of output to rise. This tendency would, on the basis of the study mentioned, be the inevitable result of wage leadership in the fastest growing sectors, so that economic growth itself could create the tendency for unit labour costs to rise.

The mechanism just described need not operate with the inevitability of clockwork. The transmission may take place the other way round – from the less productive to the more productive sectors. For example, in the autumn of 1969 industrial civil servants in the United Kingdom obtained an increase of

---

* G. Edgren, K-O. Faxén and C-E. Odhner, 'Wages, Growth and the Distribution of Income', *Swedish Journal of Economics*, September 1969.

† H. A. Turner and D. A. S. Jackson, 'On the Determination of the General Wage Level – A World Analysis; or "Unlimited Labour Forever"', *Economic Journal*, December 1970.

$8\frac{1}{2}$ per cent; dustmen and other manual workers of local authorities, whose initial claim had been for 5 per cent, received some
10 per cent. From the public sector the increases then rippled
outwards into the private sector.

The initiating causes can indeed be manifold. A more 'militant'
union leader might have come to power and, anxious to appear
different from his predecessor, might have sought and obtained
a large settlement which is widely broadcast. Whatever the
initiating cause, the increase then becomes a signal, a 'social'
standard for others to follow. The rationale often given for this
following movement is economic, the market establishing a
competitive rate; but the inspiration behind it is social and
political: each feels entitled to the increase which others, particularly those near him, are seen to be getting.

Sometimes it is not just the pay increase accruing to someone
else which is followed, but the absolute differentials in levels of
pay. A merger of one company with another will generally cause
pressure for pay in all the factories of the merged group to be
levelled up to the highest. There is no labour market in the sense
that labour moves from one factory in the group to another; but
the knowledge of higher pay in one factory sets up tension in
another. Likewise companies producing the same product in
different locations will be under pressure to pay the highest rate;
for example, automobile firms in the southern part of the
United Kingdom are under pressure to pay earnings equivalent
to those obtained in the Midlands – even though employment
conditions generally may vary from one location to another. It is
possible even that the imitative process may become international.
Airline pilots compare their pay with that paid by other airlines,
particularly with salary scales in United States airlines. It is not
too fanciful to suggest that an increase emerging from this
comparison may provide a standard for others not in airlines and
not in the United States to follow. Canada is the classic case in
point. Output per head is below that of the United States; but
social emulation of the United States causes wage increases to
follow the lead of the United States. And a union such as the
Automobile Workers' Union of the United States, which nego-
tiates with a handful of international companies in Detroit, will

have every motive to raise the level of earnings in the factories of those companies in other countries than the United States, lest otherwise competition from these countries should diminish employment in Detroit. Indeed the Automobile Workers' Union makes considerable (and successful) efforts in trying to raise the pay of car workers in countries outside the USA. It follows that the wage lead can be set not necessarily by the leading sector in one's own country, but by the economically leading country.

To verify the suggestion that wages are affected by considerations other than those normally obtaining in a market we have to probe more deeply into that much-neglected aspect, the psychology of labour. The writers of the eighteenth and early nineteenth centuries were probably on the right track when they described the worker as seeking a 'subsistence' wage or, as Marx would have it, a 'socially necessary wage'. To an age emerging from a centuries-old rural torpor during which the standard of living of the ordinary man had changed but little, it was probably true that the worker sought (economically at least) no more than that which had become essential to him from habit. That, however, is no longer the age in which we live.

The modern age is one in which progressing technology has made for constantly rising living standards, well above a traditional 'subsistence' level. In this respect the prognoses both of Ricardo and Marx are shown in retrospect to have been wrong. Since Ricardo and Marx wrote there have been great political changes. The franchise is now universal. This means that, at the very least, political rights are far more equal than they ever were previously; it would be surprising, then, if 'everyman' did not attempt to extend into the economic field the political equality to which he has become accustomed. The first economic manifestation of this exercise of a new political right was seen in the creation of the Welfare State, which nominally establishes a minimum of income below which nobody shall fall. Above the minimum there can rise a mountain of differentials. But why should somebody with a nominal political right equal to everybody else's be content just with an equal minimum? Why should he not try more insistently to try and climb the mountain? The struggle for economic equality is to the twentieth century what the struggle for political rights was to the nineteenth century. The vital question is: how smoothly can we manage the transition? The psychology which labour brings to bear upon the determination of wages cannot be divorced from this wider social and non-economic context.

Let us consider some of the ways in which this psychology may express itself. We have noted Keynes' observation that money wages were resistant to downward pressure in an economic recession. We have probably reached the stage where the level of *real* take-home pay is now resistant to downward pressure; workers, that is to say, will endeavour at least to maintain the purchasing power of their pay packets. In considering the real worth of their earnings they may take into account not only higher prices but also higher taxes, and so will respond to increased taxes by demanding higher money wages. If this is indeed so, it could have considerable implications for conventional methods of dealing with inflation, as we shall later see. Possibly even, after some twenty-five years of full employment, workers have become accustomed to a certain annual *rate of increase* in their real standards and will endeavour to maintain that rate. Nor will they react just to current events; they may even act in advance of events foreseen. They will anticipate with higher wage claims the introduction of a new tax such as a Value Added Tax or entry into the European Community with its rumoured concomitant of higher food prices, or the heralded launch of an 'incomes policy'.

Indeed it is more fruitful to view trade unions as a political movement rather than as economic monopolies, as they are depicted in purely economic writings. This is true whether they are 'reformist' Social Democratic trade unions, or Marxist trade unions; whether they have fathered a political party, as they have the Labour Party in the United Kingdom, or whether they merely lean more towards one political party than another, as they do towards the Democratic Party in the United States. Trade unions are political in that they see themselves as existing to protect and promote the interest of a class – the working class, whether this be within a system of privately owned capital, a mixed system of private and public capital, or a system of

wholly public capital. They can pursue their aims either on the
narrowly industrial front, where they are often pushed from
below; or on the broader political front, where the Welfare
State and prolonged full employment are the main post-war
achievements. Beaten on the one front, trade unions can seek to
advance on the other. Meeting with resistance on pay, as before
1939, they surge forward on the political front with full employment, as in 1945. Alternatively, faced with legislation to regulate
strikes in the United Kingdom in 1972, they pressed their wage
claims with unabated, and possibly increased, vigour. The
struggle remains essentially the same.

It is a feature of purely economic writings that they see men
behaving in markets solely as economic men, instead of seeing
men as importing into economic aspects of life aspirations that
are affected by their social and political thinking. It is this which
has led to the belief that inflation is entirely an economic phenomenon; once allowance is made for social aspects, inflation
can also be (properly) seen as a phenomenon with important
social and political roots. But immediately the question arises:
who gains? Clearly some kinds of labour gain relatively to others.
He who first gives the signal gains. If it is the workers in the most
productive sectors who set the lead, it is they who gain. Or the
workers in a sheltered sector may steal a march. There is not
necessarily a consistent pattern; often chance selects the gainer.
Once prices begin to accelerate, even those who set the pace by
way of increases in earnings may soon see the benefit reduced.
And there are some who are left permanently behind. For example, in the United Kingdom pay for a sector without an organized
labour force is set by Wages Councils sitting under an independent
Chairman and with one or two other independent members.
The percentage increases determined by these Councils tend to
follow the general pattern, though with some lag; the same
percentage increase, however, would mean that in absolute terms
a better-paid worker would obtain more than a low-paid worker;
the distance between the two would therefore be increased. Union
activity can result in modifying the flow of incomes to different
groups of wage-earners, there being no one comprehensive
explanation as to who are the main beneficiaries.

Now, in a society which is content to abide by a traditional standard of living and which is not consumed by a passion for equal increases or equal absolute levels of pay, pressures need not arise to push up earnings faster than the rate of growth in the gross national product. But in a society which is accustomed to constantly rising living standards and which seeks to imitate the largest increase in earnings that it sees around it, the tendency, as we have shown, will be for earnings to exceed the rate of increase in the gross national product and for labour costs per unit of output to rise. Such a society, for social and political rather than for economic reasons, will have an inflationary bias. Both inflation and full employment spring from the same basic cause – the assertion in the economic field of rights enjoyed in the political arena.

Individuals may assert what they regard as economic rights in their capacity as individuals. For example, individual truck drivers carrying materials to a building site where workers have secured an increase in earnings may go back to their employers and, as individuals, claim increased pay. Even without trade unions, therefore, it is possible that modern society might have an inflationary bias. The presence of trade unions accentuates that bias. Trade unions certainly can put a floor to earnings in a recession. And the extension of trade unions up the social scale, to cover, for example, white- as well as blue-collar workers, may facilitate the maintenance of pay differences between different social classes. When we talk of trade unions, however, we have to be careful about what we mean. As we saw earlier, the writers of the nineteenth century likened a trade union to a monopoly. It is doubtful, however, whether the simile goes to the heart of the problem, if, indeed, it is apt. The problem is the determination of even small numbers of men to band themselves together to assert what they regard as their rights, even though the grouping may be temporary and ad hoc, and may not necessarily constitute a formal trade union. Indeed these small informal groupings may successfully defy the authority of the trade union, a defiance exemplified in Britain by so-called 'unofficial' strikes. These groupings are the outcome of a social and political attitude.

We can thus explain the tendency for unit labour costs to rise as the assertion by men of what they see as their rights in an age of nominal political equality and, judged by historical standards, of fast economic growth. But this goes only part of the way towards explaining the rise in labour's *share* in the national income. For labour's share to rise, prices must not rise as fast as unit labour costs. Our next question must therefore be: how do price movements react to the rise in unit labour costs?

In the five years of its existence the Prices and Incomes Board dealt with some seventy-seven price cases. The situations were all highly varied. There were industries which were in the hands of one owning body offering products or services competing with other products, but which were none the less expanding, such as electricity. Equally there were industries, also in the hands of one proprietor, also in fierce competition with other products, but which were contracting, such as coal and railways. At the other extreme there were industries in which the firms were numerous but in which wages were settled collectively for the entire industry in a Wages Council, such as road haulage. There were, again, industries in which the firms were numerous but in which wages were negotiated separately between each firm and a single trade union, such as the car delivery industry. In between these two extremes there were industries with half a dozen or so firms not greatly unequal in size, such as brewing and baking; and, finally, there were industries with few firms, but with some predominant in size over the others, such as bricks and cement. In practically each and every one of these cases an increase in wages was cited as the increase in costs necessitating higher prices.

One would not wish to generalize too much on the basis of this varied experience. The maker of a product being produced under competitive conditions might choose to absorb the wage increase, cut his profit and keep his prices unchanged. Other makers of the same product would then have to follow suit. It is where there are a few makers and sellers of a product – a common condition in modern economies and known technically as 'oligopoly' – that theory would expect a price increase to follow on a general wage increase; most firms being thought to be hesitant to embark on a 'price war' and preferring to raise prices in common. This theory was borne out when, in 1965, other producers, abroad as well as in the United Kingdom, followed I C I in raising the prices of dyestuffs. But the experience of the Prices and Incomes Board was that the translation of increased wages into increased prices is more automatic than theory would lead one to believe. There may be several reasons for this. It may be that the condition of oligopoly in manufacturing is compounded by that of competition in retailing. For example, ice cream manufacturers assured the Board that there was no collaboration in pricing; but information about impending price increases inevitably spread abroad because of the large number of customers with whom price changes had to be discussed in advance. Or it may be that the appearance of competition is belied because the apparently competing firms negotiate over wages with the same trade union or set of trade unions; their response to the outcome of the negotiations tends therefore to be the same. I suspect, however, that the deeper reason for the wage–price connection is that there is an imitativeness of behaviour which operates in the field of prices just as much as it does in the field of wages. The Board's experience with prices suggests that there is an attitude which causes prices to rise whenever wages rise, even in the face of circumstances which make the onward passage of prices difficult. The attitude of management is the mirror image of the attitude of labour. Just as labour presses for higher wages when prices rise, so managements raise prices when wages rise. Just as there is wage leadership in the sense that one sector leads, and others follow, so also is there price leadership in the sense that one firm raises its price to match rising labour costs, and other firms follow. To most managements the new inflation means, not rising prices, but rising labour costs.

There is no satisfactory recent study of the structure of British industry which would allow one firmly to assess whether it is becoming more or less competitive, or to confirm whether greater competition implies higher or lower costs. But the price situations looked at by the Board did not suggest that competition is necessarily always effective in holding down prices in relation to costs. First, where there is ease of entry, as in retailing, that very fact may make for higher costs; the ease with which a small shop can be acquired or established can impede the flow of trade to a less costly supermarket and force manufacturers to raise their margins to retailers. For example, the costs of the large number of small shops through which confectionery is distributed were rising faster than the manufacturers' prices; the shopkeepers therefore pressed for higher margins to maintain their incomes. Second, in an industry which is apparently competitive the firms can either jointly, through a national wage bargain, or separately through facing the same trade union or unions incur roughly the same wage increase, which they will, all in turn, translate into a price increase. In other words, to talk only of trade union monopoly is too simple; it is the joint position of unions and firms vis-à-vis consumers which has to be considered. Third, in an industry which is dominated by one large firm, that firm may hesitate to expand its market share as much as it might lest it incur public disfavour; the price will then be set by the higher costs of smaller firms which are suffered to occupy part of the field. In such a case it is not economic power that is to be feared; it is rather the conscious restraint of power implied in the toleration of less efficient rivals. And if it be true, as the merger movement of recent years suggests, that more industries tend to become dominated by one or two large firms while still having a tail of smaller firms, then prices may increasingly reflect the higher costs of the laggards.

One reaches the same conclusions about firms' propensities to raise prices if one looks at the likely response of companies to the methods resorted to by Governments to lower the level of economic activity. These methods are monetary, in the sense of making capital more costly or more difficult to obtain, and fiscal in the sense of raising taxes on corporations or reducing tax incentives to investment. To an increased cost of capital or increased difficulty in obtaining capital, companies can respond by raising more of their required capital internally – that is by raising their prices. In effect this shifts the conventional view of prices as simply a market mechanism for allocating and rationing goods and services, according to consumers' desires, to a new view that prices form the means whereby management raises investment funds from the consuming public. This was certainly the case with the brewing companies whose application for an increase in prices was examined by the Board towards the end of 1969. Similarly companies can respond to a reduction in tax allowances or an increase in taxes more quickly than they used to in that the newer techniques of investment appraisal, which discount to their present value the cost and yield of an investment through time, specifically take into account the effect of taxes and allowances on the flow of cash in each period.

In addition to the increasing sophistication which firms apply to investment in equipment, so as to take account, for example, of the incidence of taxation over years to come, there is also the increasing sophistication which shareholders, or institutions acting on their behalf, apply to investment in stocks and shares. Just as workers seek at least to maintain, if not to increase, their real earnings after tax, that is, their net earnings in terms of what they can buy, so also it is possible that shareholders or those acting for them may try at least to maintain, if not to increase, the real net return on their portfolio investments. More important, the society of which workers and shareholders are both part must affect them in the same way and cause them to behave in a not dissimilar fashion. If workers try to claim an increasing share of the national income, so also will shareholders. Firms have to take into account the expectations of shareholders when settling the pricing policies which determine their profits. The continuing spread of more refined techniques for selecting portfolio investments suggests that this too may be giving an upward bias to prices.

To some extent this attitude may be rationalized by accountancy arithmetic. Capital-intensive methods of producing are more widespread than they used to be; so are the large staffs engaged on, for example, research. On both counts the proportion of fixed or overhead costs to total costs is probably higher than it was previously. If this is so, then a general lowering of economic activity will raise fixed costs per unit of output; the normal reaction to such an increase in unit costs will be to protect the profits by raising prices. The unit costs of the London Brick Company, for example, had risen because of an under-utilization of capacity; and the company wished to restore its rate of profit to its previous level through a substantial price increase. In other words, the prices of manufactured goods may tend to rise even in the face of falling demand.

The new inflation arises from these facts: that in a modern mass society there is a tendency for wage increases to outstrip the increases in output per man; that the resistance to the translation of these wage increases into price increases, even on the part of apparently competitive industries, is not all that great; that there may be certain long-term factors making for higher prices on grounds other than increased wages – possibly a more sophisticated computation of the long-term effect on profits of the cost of capital and of taxes and allowances, possibly a more persistent effort by shareholders to realize their expectations, possibly the determination of prices by higher rather than by lower cost firms; and that prices are more stubborn than they used to be to attempts to lower the level of economic activity.

That prices may not be all that resistant to wage costs per unit of output is borne out by Chart 5, which shows that over the last twenty or so years in the United Kingdom the price index has lagged only somewhat behind the movement in wage costs. The relationship of cause and effect could, of course, have been the other way round – price increases could have been the initiating cause and wage costs the effect. Undoubtedly this can happen. The fact, however, that over a long span of years the share of labour in the national income has increased while the pre-tax rate of profit has somewhat declined suggests that the main cause of persistently rising prices is to be found in rising wage costs per unit of output.

Some prices are less responsive to rising wage costs than others. As far as the United Kingdom is concerned, these less responsive prices are export prices. Chart 6 shows that, while export prices have also almost continuously risen, their rise has not been so steep as the rise in the prices of consumer goods. If the main cause of rising prices is to be found in rising wage costs, it may well be asked why some countries show faster rising wage costs than others. A good deal of the answer to this

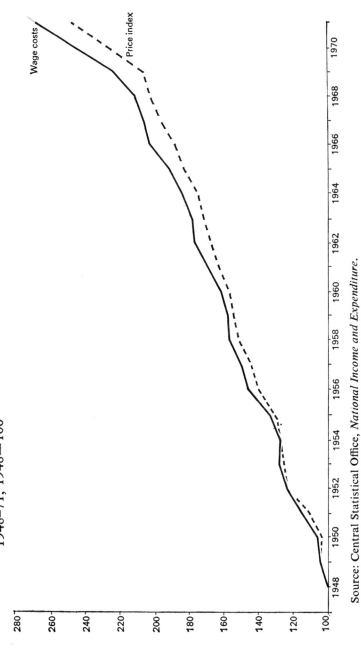

Chart 5 Wage costs per unit of output and the national income price index, 1948–71, 1948=100

Source: Central Statistical Office, *National Income and Expenditure.*

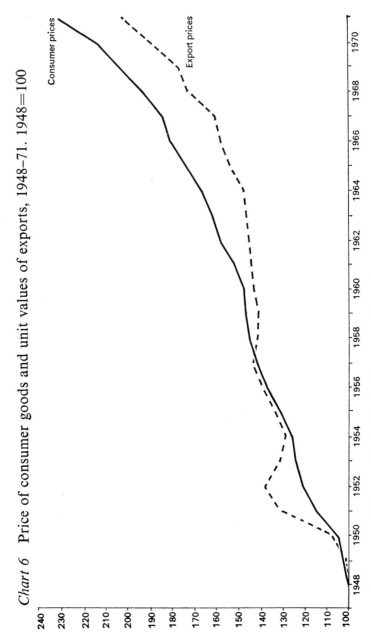

Chart 6 Price of consumer goods and unit values of exports, 1948–71. 1948=100

Source: Central Statistical Office, *National Income and Expenditure.*

question is surely to be found in different social and political backgrounds, rather than solely in differing economic circumstances.

The social tendency of wages to follow the rate of increase in productivity in the fastest-growing sectors, which we have described as the root cause of the 'new inflation', implies a close relationship between price and wage movements. Studies of the effects of prices on wages show that the impact lies in the range of 0·5 ($\pm 0·2$). In other words, some 50 per cent of any increase in the retail price index will normally be translated into wage increases. But the onward transmissipn of price increases into wage increases need not necessarily be confined to this normal figure. An unexpected jolt to prices through some such event as devaluation, causing import prices to rise, may cause a heightening of social tensions. In these tensions trade-union actions become more markedly *defensive* but are in their turn mistakenly interpreted as initiating causes of inflation. The adjustment of wages to prices quickens, so that an increase in prices can become translated into an increase in wages to the order of 100 per cent. This is the pattern of inflation to be seen in some Latin American countries. That pattern has not yet appeared in Britain, though the trend is indeed alarming. The short-term problem is to brake the momentum of inflation; the long-term problem is to ensure continued moderation in the rate of price and wage increase. This is what was meant by saying at the end of Chapter One that anti-inflation policies are here to stay. But first we should ask: what lessons can be drawn from the failures of the past?

Chapter Three

The Solutions of Conventional Wisdom

Now that we have outlined the causes which explain the move-ment of unit labour costs, a crucial factor in the process of inflation, we can consider some of the remedies resulting from conventional wisdom, the ways in which these were found to be inadequate, and the first tentative efforts that were made to supplement them with other types of policies.

A solution commonly put forward as a method of controlling inflation is for the Government to increase unemployment, supposedly more effective than any attempt by the Government to influence wages and prices 'directly'. The assumption on which this suggested alternative is based is that the lower the level or 'pressure' of total demand, the less will be the rise in incomes and prices. For the moment let us ignore such questions as the welfare of the unemployed and their dependants, or the loss to an economy if a substantial proportion of its human resources is not used. Is there in fact a choice between faster-rising prices and higher unemployment?

Higher unemployment can be brought about through a com-bination of methods. The Government may cut down on its own planned spending, thus decreasing the Government's own contribution to total demand; it may try to cut down the contribution to total demand of companies and individuals by raising taxes on the income of corporations and private citizens, and in the case of the latter by raising taxes on the goods they buy (indirect taxes); and it may make it costlier and more difficult for companies and individuals to obtain credit. The first two sets of methods may be labelled fiscal; the third method may be labelled monetary. The fiscal and the monetary methods have historically been used in conjunction with each other, though in varying degrees. Broadly speaking, in the United Kingdom main reliance has been placed on the fiscal method, while in the United States the reverse has been the case, at any rate until recently. The two methods should be used in combination, for to make credit more costly or more difficult to obtain may be in vain if the Government's own planned spending is maintained or increased, thus sustaining the Government's own contribution to total demand and conceivably the ability of the banks to grant credit.

It was seen in the last chapter that the use by Governments of certain specific instruments could indeed be thwarted by companies. In particular it was seen that taxes and allowances for investment were now being increasingly taken into account in the appraisal of investment projects and therefore presumably in the determination of prices; higher taxes or lower allowances could therefore be circumvented by higher prices; the higher prices would in their turn create pressures for increases in wages, though there is uncertainty over the extent to which this would happen and over the interval of time likely to elapse before wages were affected. Similarly it was seen that companies could react to more difficult credit conditions by relying increasingly on their own finance to maintain their investment programmes – that is, by raising their prices; once again the higher prices would to some extent be translated into higher wages. A decrease in planned Government spending, in so far as it reduced the ability of the banks to extend credit, would have a similar result – with diminished access to credit, firms could finance their investment more from their own resources by raising prices. The one Government method of increasing unemployment not so far considered is an increase in indirect taxes. This was one of the principal measures used in the United Kingdom between 1965 and 1968. The effect of higher indirect taxes in bringing about higher prices is almost immediate; and the subsequent effect in pushing up wages follows quickly, probably more quickly than in the case of any of the other measures mentioned. The very measures then resorted to by a Government to induce higher unemployment and thus, it is hoped, a slower increase in wages and prices, are themselves provocative of an increase in prices and, through prices, wages; the response, however, will be delayed. It is this delay in response which can bring about higher unemployment. Were incomes to rise quickly in answer to a Government's attempt to lower demand, demand would in fact be sustained in this way and the Government's attempts to create higher unemployment would be frustrated.

Granted that at present the Government can bring about some degree of higher unemployment, what is the level of unemployment required for prices to remain stable? Here we have to rely on estimates based on past relationships between the level of unemployment and changes in unemployment and wages. The most famous of these measures of past statistical relationships is that of Professor A. W. Phillips. Writing in 1958 he concluded that, leaving aside the complication of rising import prices, domestic prices would be stable in the United Kingdom at a level of unemployment a little under 2·5 per cent.

The most important aspect of Professor Phillips's conclusion is not so much this precise figure of 2·5 per cent (though for a time in the United Kingdom a halo of sanctity came to surround it) as the suggestion that over time there is a stable relationship between unemployment and changes in wages. But, we may argue, surely the most important qualification to be made about a study of statistical relationships going into the distant past is that institutions change and it is improbable that they change without bringing some change in psychology. For example, the reaction of wage-earners to unemployment (and, therefore, their earnings claims during periods of unemployment) probably changed with the industry-wide extension of unemployment benefit in the United Kingdom in 1920; it probably changed again with the implementation of the Redundancy Payments Act in 1965 (which made it obligatory for firms to make a lump sum payment to any worker made redundant); and yet again with the introduction in 1966 of Unemployment Benefit related to earnings. With each change it is likely that there resulted a greater readiness to 'accept' unemployment, in which case, assuming some connection between unemployment and prices, still higher unemployment than before would be required to keep prices stable.

Or, to take another example, the attitude of trade union leaders towards the maintenance of wages or of increases in wages in times of some unemployment is likely to change with spreading economic education. This argument is not quite so fanciful as it may sound. Throughout the greater part of the 1960s British trade union leaders were in regular consultation with Governments, both Conservative and Labour, about the likely rate of growth of the British economy. At the beginning of 1969 the trade union leaders thought that the (real) rate of growth might be as high as 6 per cent a year, their contention for some ten years having been that the economy could grow at a faster rate than the Government was allowing it to. The Government, anxious not to encourage too large a flood of imports and to ensure that enough capacity should be available for export, thought that a tolerable annual rate of increase might be 3 to 3·5 per cent. The dispute was never resolved, and union leaders must have gone into negotiations believing that the economy could sustain wage increases larger than those indicated by the Government as being the maximum the country could afford.

By early 1970 unemployment had increased from the post-war average of about 1·5 per cent a year to 2·7 per cent, levels of real consumption had been held almost stationary for about two years, and certainly the rate of economic growth was far below that which the trade unions thought achievable. The resulting trade union reaction was in fact to press for larger wage claims. Trade union leaders had come to learn that, to the extent to which incomes rose faster than prices, they could thereby expand consumption, expand demand, and might indeed accelerate the rate of economic growth. The attempt to hold down consumption and increase the level of unemployment was beginning to prove counter-productive.

So far, therefore, from its being true tha t increases in wages and prices are moderated by higher unemployment, the opposite may now be the case – the higher the unemployment, the more provocative it may be of wage claims. Trade unions, which we have described as essentially political in nature, have learnt enough to be able to launch a counter-attack on an attempt by Government to induce higher unemployment. Up to a point, but up to a point only, the counter-attack will nullify the Government's efforts. The qualification 'up to a point' is necessary because whatever action the Government takes the response will be delayed, and the delay will ensure for the Government an initial degree of success.

The important point is that the mechanism of the new inflation described in Chapter Two is not likely to be greatly influenced by rising unemployment if trade unions are seen as political in nature and imitative of one another. Even at a somewhat higher level of unemployment there can still take place an initial high wage settlement; that settlement may then be copied right across the country, with the result that the increase in wages per employee is greater than the increase in the gross domestic product per employee, and prices rise. Indeed, price inflation could paradoxically be aggravated by deflation because historically the rise in labour costs per unit of output has tended to be greater in phases of rising unemployment than in phases of falling unemployment; output per employee rose less when unemployment was rising, workers not being laid off at the same rate as output tailed off. However, it is true that this need not always be so and it is possible that as far as the United Kingdom is concerned the last few years represent a departure from the pattern, output per head having risen with rising unemployment.

To suggest that higher unemployment is an alternative to some Governmental attempt to influence directly the course of prices and incomes rests on two dubious assumptions: first, that at a higher level of unemployment labour costs per unit of output will rise more slowly than would otherwise be the case; second, that a mass electorate will more readily accept higher unemployment than some Governmental attempt to influence the course of prices and incomes. With regard to the first proposition I have given reasons for believing that, even with some increase in unemployment, labour costs may rise as sharply as, if not more sharply than, before; indeed a recession now affects the balance of payments simply by lowering the level of economic activity, but it may, in the long run, worsen the country's cost structure in relation to that of other countries. Over the longer term the balance of payments problem is not thereby solved. As for the second proposition, that a mass electorate will accept higher unemployment more readily than it will a Governmental attempt to influence the course of prices and incomes, there is no case where electors, having savoured full employment, have then allowed a Government to retreat from it in any significant measure. Since both an imitativeness in wage claims and full employment represent an assertion in the economic field of what are regarded as political rights, one must expect resistance to a fall in employment to be as strong as resistance to a lower wage increase than somebody else's.

An even more detached form of 'demand' management advocated by some relates to the money supply only. The money supply, it is said, might be more tightly controlled or its expansion might take place at a pre-determined rate, say 3 per cent a year. If the potential capacity to produce were rising at that rate then, it is argued, prices would somehow remain stable. The thesis merits mention only because it is an old doctrine revived in a new form. The concept of the supply of money is an elusive one. What matters from the point of view of the firm or the individual is the ability to command *credit*. The effects on individual firms of a tightening of the rules by the money-supplying authorities will differ. Some will be able to demand quicker payment from those who buy from them and delay payment to those from whom they buy; in this way they will get round the rules. Some will be able to get round them by raising their prices and so maintaining their ability to command credit. In short, there is no assurance that those hit first by a tightening of the rules will be those whose behaviour in prices and incomes sets a pattern for others. Again, there is no indication of how such monetary restriction will bear on the economic and social mechanism of emulative wage increases. A tightening of the supply of money is not, therefore, in itself a solution to the problem of rising prices.

Further, the contention that the money supply should be allowed to grow at a fixed rate corresponding to the rate of increase in potential output presupposes a stable starting-point, in the sense that neither is output thought to be too low (and therefore unemployment too high) nor are prices considered to be rising too fast; thereafter, the thinking would run, a stable relationship could continue between output and prices. The starting-point is in fact seldom stable: either output is thought to be too low (and unemployment too high), or prices are considered to be rising too fast, or both unacceptable volumes of output (and unemployment) and intolerable inflation exist together. Nor, assuming a stable starting-point, is the subsequent relationship between output and prices likely to remain stable with a fixed rate of increase in the money supply. We have seen that an increasing proportion of the total output or the national income has gone to labour, and that prices rising faster than output largely reflect this fact.

An escape from rising prices or at any rate from the balance of payments difficulties caused by prices rising faster than in other countries is sometimes suggested in the shape of a floating exchange rate. One country may be more careless than another in its attitude towards prices because its folk memory may be different; a country with a memory of unemployment, such as the United Kingdom, may be more careless than a country with a memory of inflation, such as West Germany. With a floating rate of exchange, the rate of the pound sterling would on this analysis tend continuously to fall and the the prices of its imports to rise. The question then is whether the chain of events would cause the attitudes of trade unions to change or not. There is no means of being certain about this. The experience might prove so traumatic that attitudes would indeed change and a greater care thereafter be shown towards rising prices. But it is far more likely that increases in import prices would merely stimulate even more vigorous wage demands, and so defeat the floating rate. There would then follow a continuing depreciation in the rate of exchange. All we can say for certain is that a continuously depreciating exchange rate is a symptom of inflation; it is not a cure.

The solutions to the problem of inflation so far described may be termed 'macro-economic' solutions. That is to say, they attempt to damp down inflation by reducing or by changing total demand in the economy in relation to the total potential output. They do so by reducing the Government's share of demand through lower Government spending, by reducing private demand through higher taxes, or by reducing both public and private demand through squeezing the supply of money. The solution of a floating exchange rate tries to change the composition of total demand – lowering the demand for imports and increasing the demand for exports. Reasons have been given for suggesting that attemps to control or to deflect the impact of inflation by regulating both the total level and the composition of demand are likely in practice to fail. Recent history bears out this view as far as the total level of demand is concerned. Attempts to change the composition of demand through a floating exchange rate are new, most countries having attempted since the Bretton Woods Agreement to maintain fixed rates of exchange, though even in this area recent events carry a lesson.

That macro-economic policies are not enough, that they have at least to be supplemented by something else, is indicated by the intensified attempts which have been made to change the structure of trade unions and firms, or to influence the bargaining relationships which are thought to determine wages and prices. For example, the Royal Commission on Trade Unions and Employers' Associations (the Donovan Commission) reporting in June 1968, saw the problem of industrial relations in the United Kingdom (and therefore by extension the problem of incomes rising faster than output) as being one of 'fragmented bargaining' within factories; that is, bargaining was often a process of 'leap-frogging' or of competition for higher earnings between different factories within one company, or between different groups within one factory.

It saw the remedy in part in the conclusion of 'comprehensive agreements' for companies and/or factories, in the amendment of national agreements to make possible more realistic factory and company agreements, and in 'many more mergers between unions'. The Donovan Commission's analysis of the problem coincides very much with the theory of 'wage leadership' and with experience of the Prices and Incomes Board: namely, that emulation between factory groups and between unions makes for the levelling-up or the 'bidding-up' of pay increases to the increase obtained by the highest. However, its prescription of a solution, namely plant and company bargaining, could mean that the working of the wage leadership mechanism was merely transferred to another plane without much change in the nature of the problem.

The publication of the Donovan Report was followed in January 1969 by the publication of the Labour Government's White Paper *In Place of Strife* (Cmnd 3888) which set out the action proposed by the Government as a result of the Donovan recommendations. In certain respects the action proposed went beyond the Donovan Report: in particular the Government suggested that it should hold a reserve power to secure a 'conciliation' pause where there was a threatened strike in breach of the procedure agreed upon between employer and union, and a similar discretionary power to require a union to hold a ballot on the question of strike action. There ensued a controversy, the echoes of which will long be heard, as to whether agreements between employers and unions on the procedures to be followed in disputes between them should be enforceable at law (as they are in the United States and other countries) or whether they should remain untouched by law. The successor Conservative Government did in fact later succeed in putting a law on the statute book – the Industrial Relations Act of 1971. The intention of this law was to define as 'unfair industrial practices' strikes by unions which were non-registered (that is, which did not register with the appropriate authority) or strikes called by unauthorised representatives of registered unions. A newly created court, the National Industrial Relations Court, could then make orders prohibiting such unfair practices and could also award compensation to the wronged party. Both *In Place of Strife* and the Industrial Relations Act sought to blunt the weapon of strikes, but without removing it. Both, therefore, can be said to have tried to deal with trade unions as monopolies. Neither went to the root of inflation.

The converse of such policies for trade unions is an anti-monopoly policy for businesses. But of its own accord this will not provide a solution to the problem of inflation. Not that there would be many who would express objection to the existence of such a law. Even if anti-trust laws have done little historically to stem the tide towards larger companies, they have the merit of instilling caution in the behaviour of dominant enterprises. But, as said earlier, that very caution may then lead to the toleration of higher cost companies; it is these which can then determine prices. Attempts to 'atomize' firms and trade unions, seek to restore concepts that are narrowly economic and hark back to the past. They do not suffice to overcome the current reality of the productivity-wage-price spiral.

There are those who believe that there is a magic palliative for inflation – namely, higher productivity. Higher output per employee could be seen as the painless and ideal way to answer rising unit labour costs; a seemingly 'positive' solution contrasted with the 'negative' solution of curbs on pay. There is nobody who does not desire higher productivity – that is to say, a higher rate of increase in the gross domestic product, provided some regard is paid to the effect of growth on the environment. What matters from the point of view of abating inflation, however, is that such productivity growth should not lead to rapid wage increases in a leading sector. There will, for inevitable reasons of differing rates of advance in technology, be differences in rates of productivity growth among industries. So that, if it be a feature of fast growth that some industries grow more rapidly than others and thus set a pattern in incomes for others, incomes will, through wage leadership, continue to outstrip the average rise in productivity. Paradoxically, a 'positive' growth policy may make a 'negative' policy of restraint even more necessary.

We are forced to the conclusion that what is required is not just macro-economic policies, nor policies dealing with strikes, monopolies and productivity. We must search elsewhere. Indeed we can trace the history of the search from the Second World War onwards. The post-war problem of continually rising prices was seen with prescience and clarity in the famous British White Paper of May 1944 entitled *Employment Policy* (Cmd 6527) in which the National Government pledged itself to 'the maintenance of a high and stable level of employment after the war'. Also foreseen was the powerlessness of Government to cope alone with the continuing inflation likely to be associated with high employment. The preview of the next twenty-five years given in that White Paper was all the more remarkable in that high employment had been experienced for only some four abnormal wartime years, years in which the Government's efforts 'to prevent a runaway rise of prices' had been fortified by 'such means as high taxation and encouragement of war savings, rationing of food and clothing, allocation of materials, control over the employment of labour and direct control of prices'.

The method by which Government could maintain employment was simple – it could maintain the level of demand. But, as the White Paper stated: 'Action taken by the Government to maintain expenditure will be fruitless unless wages and prices are kept reasonably stable'. Note the parity of emphasis on both wages and prices. The requirements on both counts were succinctly put and in close conjunction the one with the other. First, on wages: '. . . it will be essential that employers and workers should exercise moderation in wages matters so that increased expenditure provided at the onset of a depression may go to increase the volume of employment'. Second, on prices: 'An undue increase in prices due to causes other than increased wages might similarly frustrate action taken by the Government to maintain employment. If, for example, the manufacturers in a particular industry were in a ring for the purpose of raising prices, additional money made available by Government action for the purpose of maintaining employment might simply be absorbed in increased profit margins and no increase in employment would result'. Then again the refrain that Government could not do all: 'If . . . the cost of living is . . . kept stable it must be regarded as the duty of both sides of industry to consider together all possible means of preventing a rise in the costs of production or distribution and so avoiding the rise in prices which is the initial step in the inflationary process' – though why it should be a rise in prices which was the initial step and not a rise in wages was not made clear.

The only respect in which the 1944 White Paper was possibly not far-sighted enough was that it did not indicate that, once Government had given people a taste of high or full employment it was likely thereafter to be stuck with it and would be kept to it, either through the ballot box or through wage claims which employers would concede in the reasonable certainty that they could recoup them through higher prices, for the wage concessions themselves would constitute the purchasing power to sustain demand.

The theme of the limitations of Government was faintly echoed after the Second World War in White Papers published under the aegis of both Labour and Conservative Governments. Thus, for example, the immediate post-war Labour Government, in a White Paper entitled *Statement on the Economic Considerations affecting Relations between Employers and Workers* (Cmd 7018, January 1947), drew attention to its dilemma in expanding social improvements while making good wartime damage, and indicated that the dilemma could be resolved only by improvements in the productivity of British industry, improvements which 'are not the responsibility of the Government alone but of industrial management and workers alike'. A year later in a *Statement on Personal Incomes, Costs and Prices* (Cmd 7321, February 1948) the same Government declared roundly: '... until more goods and services are available for the home market, there is no justification for any *general* increase of individual money incomes ... if, notwithstanding these considerations, remuneration is increased in any class of employment, whether in private industry or under a public authority, there can be no presumption, whatever may have been the practice in the past, that the resulting costs will be taken into account in settling controlled prices, charges or margins or other financial matters requiring Government action'. The wartime apparatus of statutory price control was then still in being; and what the Government was in effect saying was that it would seek to influence the movement of wages through the constraint on prices. This was something of a departure from the parity of emphasis on wages and prices contained in the 1944 White Paper; it was also a position to which the United Kingdom was tending to return nearly twenty-five years later.

The 1948 *Statement on Personal Incomes, Costs and Prices*, in addition to looking to statutory price control to ensure that there was no general increase in money incomes, nailed its hopes to traditional 'collective bargaining'. 'The value of the system of collective bargaining', it was stated, 'and the justification for its maintenance at the present time rest upon the assumption that the terms of collective agreements will be observed loyally by all employers and workers, and the Government cannot stress too highly the importance which they attach to this principle.' Presumably what was meant by the expression 'collective bargaining' was the common British practice of industry-wide agreements between trade unions and associations of employers. If this is indeed what the authors of the Statement had in mind, then they seemed not fully to appreciate that under the influence of high employment there had begun to mushroom an irrepressible growth of disorderly factory bargaining and that twenty years later the Donovan Commission on Trade Unions was to describe the main trait of British industrial relations as 'fragmented' bargaining on the shop floor. One of the pillars on which the Government was relying for stability in prices had already begun to disintegrate.

Five years after its return to power in 1951 the first post-war Conservative Government took up, in its turn, the task of trying to enlighten the public on the problem 'of continually rising prices'. It did so in a White Paper entitled *The Economic Implications of Full Employment* (Cmnd 9725, March 1956). This White Paper described it as the Government's job 'to keep the pressure [of demand] right', not too strong, and not too weak, for 'the pressure of demand will itself contribute to forcing up prices'. But then there was added this significant sentence: 'Prices can also be forced up by pressure for higher incomes even when the level of demand is not excessive.' That sentence contained the beginning of a perception that the control of demand might indeed be wrested from the hands of Government through a race for higher incomes. It was not elaborated upon, but the message was left quite clear that 'if general price stability is to be maintained', action was required both by the Government and people, and the requisite action by the people lay in 'self-restraint in making wage claims and fixing profit margins and prices'.

In the opinion of both Labour and Conservative Governments,

then, some action was required by those whom they governed –
restraint by employees in their claims for incomes and by firms
in their determination of prices and, through prices, profits.
How were these two sets of people to do what did not come to
them naturally? For trade union leaders were supposed to get
the maximum they could for their members and certainly to copy
the best that other trade union leaders might be getting; while
economic theory held that all firms, except those operating in an
extreme form of competition seldom encountered in real life,
sought to 'maximize' their profit.

The first post-war Labour Government talked directly to the
trade union leaders. It had some title to do so. The Labour Party
was, after all, the child and the political arm of the trade union
movement; there was still in being the legacy of wartime price
control to give backing to its appeal for restraint in incomes; and
the spokesman for the Government, namely the Chancellor of
the Exchequer, Sir Stafford Cripps, recognizably possessed moral
integrity and authority. The Government was, therefore, able to
reach specific agreement with the trade unions. For the two years
1948–49 the policy worked; national wage settlements did indeed
show the moderation asked for. But two developments brought
about the collapse of the effort (it never acquired a label such as
'pause' or 'freeze' as did later efforts). The first was the growing
importance under full employment of shop-floor bargaining and
the growth in the earnings of workers paid according to piecework or output as against that of those paid according to time
worked, the latter being mainly those whose earnings reflected
the nation-wide settlement and contained little more. The
second was the rise in import prices caused initially by post-war
reconstruction and later aggravated by the devaluation of the
pound sterling in September 1949, and the outbreak of the Korean
war in June 1950. Thus the episode failed to observe the parity
of treatment between prices and incomes which had been the
hallmark of the 1944 White Paper; it also failed to observe parity
of treatment between different categories of incomes; as a result
it came to lose the appearance of equity and with that loss the
pressure for higher incomes was intensified. That these developments took place was no reflection on Sir Stafford Cripps or

necessarily on the policy which he had adopted; the 1948 White Paper had shown little awareness of the fact that shop stewards in the factory were moving out of the control of national trade union leaders; and even had he appreciated this fact Cripps could scarcely have spoken to myriads of shop stewards. What mattered for the longer term was not so much that the episode, after an initial success, had broken down, but that the reasons for the breakdown should be taken into account in future efforts. We shall see that they were not.

The next attempt was by a Conservative Chancellor of the Exchequer, Mr Harold Macmillan. In 1956, he tried to deal with the 'rolling' problem of prices stimulating wage demands, or alternatively wage increases affecting prices, by instituting what was called a 'plateau'. The 'plateau' was, however, confined to public sector prices, and employers in the private sector felt let down because there was no attempt to deal with public sector wages thought to be under the Government's influence.

Mr Macmillan's successor as the Chancellor of the Exchequer, Mr (as he then was) Peter Thorneycroft, had to do more than just maintain a 'plateau' for prices and incomes in the public sector; somehow or other he had to affect the private sector. How was he to do it? To talk, as Sir Stafford Cripps had done, directly to the trade unions would not do, for the Conservative Party had no link with the trade unions; and despite the presence of a placatory Minister of Labour in Sir Walter Monckton the trade unions could say that they had been alienated in the early fifties by the dismantling of the war-time apparatus of price control and subsidies, though some dismantling was probably inevitable. Mr Thorneycroft was not thus fortified, as Sir Stafford Cripps had been, in talking with trade union leaders. In these circumstances he set up in August 1957 an external body independent of the Government known as the Council on Prices, Productivity and Incomes (colloquially known as 'The Three Wise Men'). Whether he knew it or not, Mr Thorneycroft was taking the first step in reversing some 150 years or more of constitutional history.

In the seventeenth and eighteenth centuries Government, broadly speaking, had been conducted by boards or commissions, for example, the Commissioners of Customs and Excise, the heads of which were Ministers of the Crown, belonged to neither Tories nor Whigs, but none the less were members of the House of Commons. In the nineteenth century, with the extension of the franchise, and the increased assertion by Parliament of its power vis-à-vis the monarch, the Boards or Commissions, for example the Board of Trade, developed into Departments of Government, with their heads, the Ministers, the members of a party, and their officials serving them no matter to which party the Ministers belonged. Mr Thorneycroft was now entrusting to an outside Commission a task which had constitutionally become one of the Government's own prerogatives. The reasons behind this change are one of the main concerns of this book.

Thus, a search was afoot for something additional to conventional macro-economic policies to provide a solution to the problem of inflation: this was to involve a *general* direct restraint in prices and incomes.

Consider the extremely general terms of reference given to 'The Three Wise Men'. They were: 'Having regard to the desirability of full employment and increasing standards of life based on expanding production and reasonable stability in prices, to keep under review changes in prices, productivity and the level of incomes (including wages, salaries and profits) and to report thereon from time to time'. To emphasize the general nature of the terms of reference Mr Peter Thorneycroft said in the House of Commons on 25th July 1957 that the Council 'is not concerned with specific wage claims or disputes'. 'Our hope', he said, 'is that it [the Council] will create a fuller appreciation of the facts, both in the public at large and amongst those more immediately concerned with prices and cost matters.' The very generality of these terms of reference almost amounted to an invitation to the Council to comment on general economic policy. This is what happens in, for example, West Germany, and there can indeed be a case for independent comment on economic policy to help a Government pursue a strait economic course even on the eve of an appeal to the electorate. Be that as it may, comment on economic policy in general is what the Council initially did. Starting from a position which the Government had in part abandoned in the 1956 White Paper, the Council, in its first report published in February 1958, saw the cause of the rise in prices and incomes in 'an abnormally high level of demand ... for an abnormally long stretch of time'. But by the time of the fourth report, which appeared in July 1961, a change had occurred. The Council observed that 'experience has shown tha removing excess demand was not of itself enough ... inflation has another cause, an upward push as rates of pay are raised and profit margins are maintained by rising prices'. At the heart of the problem of inflation and of full employment was a frame of mind. After five years the Council had come back to what the Government had begun to perceive in the White Paper of 1956 – namely, that to remove excess demand was not enough.

Even if the trade unions had not been predisposed in favour of a body established by a Conservative Government, the emphasis placed in the Council's first two reports on the removal of excessive demand (that is, on an implied increase in unemployment) would have cemented trade union antagonism towards it. Nor indeed, in the light of trade union opposition, was the Council able to survive.

The Government's preoccupation with prices and incomes did not, however, cease with the publication of the Council's last report. On the contrary, on 25 July 1961 the Chancellor of the Exchequer, now Mr Selwyn Lloyd, announced a 'wage pause' for Government employees, and the 'pause' was later extended to workers covered by Wages Councils. Nor did the Government cease to think it desirable to be able to lean on some external body. The body, however, became two, if not indeed three. The broad function of surveying the economic scene which had in a sense been discharged by the 'Three Wise Men' was, as from March 1962, performed by a new body known as the National Economic Development Council (colloquially known as 'Neddy'). Chaired by the Chancellor of the Exchequer and with the attendance of other Ministers, the new Council consisted of representatives both of management and of trade unions. And it was to be served by an office which would be semi-independent of the Government, known as the National Economic Development Office (NEDO). The most noteworthy feature of the new Council was the participation in its proceedings of trade union leaders, and there is some evidence that in 'bargaining' their way on to the Council they secured an end to the 'wage pause' on 1 April 1962. The Government had thus secured a forum in which the general economic problems of the country could be discussed, and potentially wages too, but it had lost its 'wage pause'.

Almost simultaneously with the formation of the National Economic Development Council there was established, in November 1962, the National Incomes Commission. This was to consist entirely of independent members in the sense that they were not members of the Government nor employers nor trade union leaders, though they were appointed by the Government, and its function was to consider, on reference to it by the Government, specific wage claims or settlements. As distinct from the general subjects previously handled by The Three Wise Men and now to be handled by the National Economic Development Council, the National Incomes Commission was to deal with *specific* cases. The formation of the National Incomes Commission was thus a watershed. There was no link between the Council and the National Incomes Commission, and the trade unions, while being represented on the first, would have nothing to do with the second. Broad guidance on the matter of incomes was given to the Commission not by the Council, but by the Government, whose spokesmen, according to the Commission, advised it that the likely growth in the national product and therefore the appropriate guide for pay increases was 2 to $2\frac{1}{2}$ per cent a year. The Commission of its own will, having heard evidence from the National Institute of Economic and Social Research, adopted what it regarded as the more realistic range of 3 to $3\frac{1}{2}$ per cent. The Commission produced four reports, three of them on pay settlements already concluded. Its title contained no allusion to prices, nor was any price reference given to it. It did, however, indirectly consider prices when assessing the impact of an increase in wages in the engineering industry. The Purchasing Officers Association complained of the resulting price increases and was invited to give evidence, but the Commission largely exonerated the industry on this indictment. In practice therefore the National Incomes Commission and the policy which it was to help prosecute did not reflect that parity of emphasis on prices and incomes which had featured so strongly in the 1944 White Paper.

On the arrival of the Labour Party to power in October 1964 a fresh start was made with an attempt by Government to affect the course of prices and incomes in general and to do so by influencing *particular* prices and incomes. It was more persistent in the sense that it lasted longer than any of its predecessors. And it forms the main theme of this book: that the creation of the Prices and Incomes Board was an inevitable outcome of historical trends already clearly manifest.

Chapter Four

The Government's Need
for New Institutions

We have described an evolution in anti-inflationary policies from a reliance by Government solely on macro-economic policies, which try indirectly to affect the course of prices and incomes, to supplementary Governmental attempts directly to influence prices and incomes, initially in a very *general* way, and later through the examination of *specific* instances. We also saw that this gradual evolution was accompanied by the rise and fall of new institutions. The economic problem lying behind these developments was inflation. But there was also a political problem. The word 'political' in this context covers two things: first, the Government's problem in dealing with its own narrower accounting, particularly the salaries paid to its own employees and the prices it charges for the goods for which it assumes responsibility – such as farm produce and the products of nationalized industries; second, the Government's attitude before a mass democracy on the deeper issues of justice and privilege which are the battleground of politics.

   Much of the activity of Government relies heavily on labour; administration is obviously a labour-intensive activity. True, as in other walks of life, capital can up to a point be substituted for labour – for example, computers for clerks; but in the case of public authorities, the scope for this may be more limited than elsewhere. In addition, the field of governmental activity has greatly expanded; whether it should have expanded in the way it has is a matter which the political parties may dispute; but the expansion is undeniable. It has followed in part on the fact that as the Government has increasingly become responsible for such services as education and health, the demand for these has grown and the provision has had to be extended too. The expansion of

Government activity in all directions is something which the present book will have to take for granted, though it is undoubtedly a phenomenon to which people have ambivalent attitudes – wanting it because it brings services not otherwise within reach, and disliking it because of the toll it levies by way of taxes on incomes.

Both because of the labour-intensive nature of Government and the enlargement of Government activity, the wage and salary bill of the public sector has greatly increased and now matters enormously in the life of the nation. The Government is now not only the direct employer of civil servants, judges, etc., but it also influences in the United Kingdom the pay of doctors, dentists and most categories of teachers, not to mention the employees of the nationalized industries. Indeed, of the country's total labour force, over one quarter consists either of the Government's own employees or of those for whose pay the Government is in some way responsible. How, in these circumstances, is the Government to determine the pay increases for which it is regarded as assuming responsibility? It has to seek a method which is acceptable to the public, appears fair to the employees for whom it is seen to be responsible, while at the same time recognizing that the scope of its own activity is such that its settlements may be regarded as a key factor in the process of wage and salary determination. These are difficult straits through which to steer a true course. If the Government concedes a high pay increase to its own employees or to those whose pay it closely affects, it is both followed and blamed by the private sector. Its dominant position overrides everything else. If, on the other hand, in seeking to ensure fairness for public employees it automatically follows some outside indicator of pay, its wage and salary bill is determined by others than itself and a good deal of its spending then escapes its own control, at a time when such control may be vital to economic stability.

As the activity of Government has been extended, so also in the United Kingdom has increased reliance been placed on some outside indicator to determine the pay of Government officials. In 1923 the Anderson committee on the civil service considered that, in the determination of civil service pay, regard should be had to 'what is necessary to recruit and retain an efficient staff'. The criterion, in other words, was economic. By 1955 the Priestley Commission on the Civil Service had laid it down that 'the primary principle of civil service pay is fair comparison with the current remuneration of outside staffs employed on broadly comparable work, taking account of differences in other conditions of service'. The criterion had shifted to one of equity. The principle of 'fair comparison' means that, if in the private sector pay has increased faster than the gross domestic product, the Government has then to follow, thus increasing its own spending and compounding the inflation. It is scarcely surprising that Governments have tried to insulate themselves against this result. They have done so by reserving in the last resort a right to determine pay unilaterally rather than see its determination through bilateral negotiation or even arbitration. Thus the document, *Staff Relations in the Civil Service* issued by HM Treasury in 1958, stated: 'The Government has not surrendered, and cannot surrender, its liberty of action in the exercise of its authority and the discharge of its responsibilities in the public interest.' Similarly the Arbitration Agreement between the Government and the civil service unions allows the Government to refuse arbitration on 'grounds of policy'. Both of these safeguards testify to the reluctance of a Government to being forced to do what the private sector has done, particularly when it deems the actions of the private sector to be wrong. It is doubtful, however, whether the safeguards are enough against the broad commitment to follow the private sector; and indeed they have been used only spasmodically. This very insufficiency forces the Government to undertake a new role – to attempt directly to influence the course of pay in the private sector.

The facts so far discussed – namely, that what the State pays its officials can be determined by the private sector – illustrate a point of wider importance. An individual in a modern society receives two kinds of income: a private income from his work and/or his savings; and an income from the State in money or in kind – in money if it is an unemployment benefit or a State pension, and in kind if it is free education for his children or free access to medical care. A Government's ability to provide what it considers is expected of it, or what it is committed to, by way of a State income in money or in kind, can be weakened by an undue increase in incomes in the private sector; a Government has then either to expand its planned spending programme in sympathy with what is happening in the private sector; for example, on pensions to keep them in line with the cost of living; or it can keep to its planned spending only by retrenching where it had not planned to retrench – for example, on housing or defence. Likewise from the point of view of the individual the fulfilment of his expectations of a State income as expressed through the ballot box can be thwarted by his demands for private income on the shop floor or round the negotiating table, and what he regards as his political freedom can be frustrated by the manner in which he exercises what he considers to be his economic freedom. There is no longer, if indeed there ever was, a neat distinction between the State or public sector and the private sector; the evolution of the first is closely dependent on events in the second; and the proper management of the first requires some influence over the second.

Just as a Government has to determine the pay of its officials, so also it has to determine the prices of certain goods – for example, those produced by industries it owns, such as, in the United Kingdom, all fuels but oil. In the determination of these prices it finds itself in much the same dilemma as that in which it finds itself in determining the pay of its officials. If it concedes large increases in the prices of such basic products as coal and electricity, the private sector seizes upon these as an occasion for raising its own prices; and the Government becomes an object of blame. If, on the other hand, the Government denies price increases, it may have to countenance large deficits by the industries concerned and may have to increase its own borrowing in order to cover them. By and large Governments in the United Kingdom have tended to opt for the second of these two courses. Whether in so doing their action has been more inflationary than if prices had been increased no one knows; there is no satisfactory analysis of the relative inflationary effects of increased prices for basic products produced, say, by nationalized industries, as against those of increased borrowing by the Government designed to cover deficits by those industries. In so far as the choice is difficult and the bias of the decisions taken has been towards holding down prices in the public sector at the cost of borrowing more to cover the resulting deficits, there is a case for finding some new mechanism to help reach and get accepted a more balanced decision. And the case is strengthened if the Government is trying to affect the course of prices in the private sector – for example, the prices determined by monopolies. The Government has then to give the appearance of fairness by subjecting the pricing of its own monopoly industries to the same kind of scrutiny.

Finally, there arise those fundamental issues of politics – justice and privilege. Perhaps the entire history of Government can be summed up as a struggle between the retention of authority by those governing against an increasing denial of authority by those governed. In the nineteenth and early twentieth centuries the broader masses of men increasingly captured the citadels of authority; while authority itself voluntarily withdrew from the economic field. The withdrawal of authority from the economic field follows logically from the concept of a market as first developed by Adam Smith towards the end of the eighteenth century and as elaborated over the next 150 years. If it indeed be true that there are markets in products and in men, and that in these markets prices and wages emerge which any one individual is powerless to affect, so small is he in relation to the total, then enormous consequences flow: there will be a political order in which each can pursue his private interest without hurt to the public interest, and the exercise of authority by Government can be minimal; there will also be a natural order the results of which are not determined by men but by mysterious things outside them, such as the laws of supply and demand; if men attempt to break these laws a certain inevitability awaits them, not quite the same inevitability of development as in Marxist thought, but an inevitability none the less – the inevitability of unemployment, for example, or to use current technical parlance, a 'natural' rate of unemployment which alone is consistent with stable prices.

Suppose, however, that the initial premise is untrue. Suppose that some groups are more powerful than others: suppose that some workers can capture for themselves the benefits of rapidly rising productivity in their industries; suppose that strong social forces exist to 'generalize' such a wage increase; suppose that trade unions operating in a field such as electricity supply demand of the Government a wage increase on pain of denying electricity to large cities; suppose that firms are quick to pass on to the consumer the burden of rising costs; suppose that trade unions jointly react to an attempt by Government to curtail demand by claiming higher wages deliberately to maintain demand. Suppose, alternatively, that the initiating movement is on the side of management: that sectors in which productivity is rising fast show exceptionally high profits, that the dividend expectations of the shareholders are raised, that firms which have a large share of the market for a product raise their prices to finance their investment, and that all this has an effect on wage claims. Then this is no longer a moral order in which each can pursue his private interest without hurt to the public interest. Nor is it a natural order in which men are the victims of events outside them; men or groups of men have a strong influence on the course of events. Nor finally is it a political order in which the exercise of authority by Government need be minimal; it is an order in which Government has difficulty in exercising any authority at all. This is surely the true contemporary position. Only now are we seeing the full result of those twin developments of the nineteenth century – the capture of political authority by the broader masses and the simultaneous diminution of public intervention in the economic sphere. Contemporary Government then is powerful – it commands an influential public sector; but it is also powerless – it faces powerful private bodies, for example, trade unions, firms, which can frustrate its operations and put its policies in jeopardy. How does it resolve this dilemma? The institutions created to deal with pay and prices, the rise and fall of which we briefly described in the last chapter, represent part of the search for an answer. Here we must probe more deeply into the nature of the answer required.

Nearly all modern Governments of a European type have developed from a common origin; the original models were characterized by an attempt to effect a balance between political authority and the powerful representative institutions of the day – they would be called nowadays 'pressure groups'. There was a monarchy balanced by a second chamber of landowning barons, by a first chamber of lesser landowners and merchants, and finally by an international church. The monarchy has now either disappeared or, where it still exists, has lost its governing powers. The church, for its part, whether international or, as in the United Kingdom, national, no longer affects temporal authority. The long and painful retreat from power of both monarchy and church has been accompanied by the acquisition of power by political parties. Nominally this power is 'exercised' by the people, who either elect a Legislature from which the Government is derived, as in most of Western Europe, or alternatively elect both a Legislature and an Administration, as in the United States. The United States constitution, being written and therefore echoing a past, still attempts a 'balance of power' between the different facets of political authority – the executive, the legislative and the judicial. It is not a balance between political authority and the other institutions of society. The present day constitution of the United Kingdom contains less of a balance than that of the United States – the Legislature, that is, Parliament, is in theory supreme, while the Executive dominates it in practice. The Legislature contains the representatives of electors voting in their capacity as individual citizens. But its composition no longer reflects the principal institutions of the day, which are now economic – namely, businesses and trade unions. The increasing scope and amount of legislation has tended to turn the task of the legislator into a full-time job. A trade union leader would certainly find it difficult to combine membership of the Legislature with active trade union leadership, and the better trade unionist tends to aspire to the role of trade union leader; while the full-time executive of the modern corporation cannot in practice be a member of the Legislature. A Government derived from the Legislature thus suffers from a double disadvantage: it is seldom nowadays manned by Ministers who have close contact with trade unions and business, and it does not find in Parliament a forum for discourse with trade unions and firms. The new organizations which the British Government created and dissolved in the fifties and sixties represented in part an attempt to find outside Parliament a vehicle for conducting just such a dialogue; and they appeared and disappeared because Government, while needing them, also feared a possible derogation from its authority or from that of the Parliament from which it sprang.

In the fifties the 'Three Wise Men' came and went. They came because Government (a Conservative Government) wanted some 'independent' support for its attempt to bring home to trade unions and firms, but trade unions in particular, the facts of economic life. The fact that they came implied an admission by a Conservative Government at any rate that it might be regarded as biased in its presentation of the national economic problem. They went because their solution to the problem still remained confusedly with macro-economic policies, while the Executive, appreciating the failures, was coming round to the view that different solutions were required.

The 'Three Wise Men' were not looked to as an extra-Parliamentary aid to the formulation of an economic plan. Such developments came only later. In the early nineteen-sixties British industrialists, searching for a means of accelerating the United Kingdom's slow rate of economic growth compared with that of other countries, began to argue the need for an 'economic plan'. The model cited was French 'indicative' planning. On the morrow of the war, French economic planning was preoccupied with the problem of post-war reconstruction and with the marshalling of priorities for this task. The problem was thus not unlike that of the largely agricultural countries of Eastern Europe consciously endeavouring to industrialize themselves. In both cases the basic industries were publicly owned. This fact alone gave to the targets set for such industries an authority which could not be entirely evaded. As industrial development proceeds, however, the emphasis shifts from the setting of objectives for basic industries to one of determining the nature and the value of investment for industries catering for consumers' needs. This much more complicated task lessens the degree of authority attaching to the total plan; and so such 'indicative' planning can be acceptable to the private sector. Indeed by coordinating investment decisions, firms may be spared the problem of creating excess capacity; in other words 'indicative' planning can give results similar to those which would emerge from long-term collusion among large firms.

This does not, however, invalidate the need for an institution outside politics. In any modern country the public sector, proportionately to the entire economy, is large, whether or not there is a large measure of public ownership of industry. A Government therefore has to attempt to evaluate the resources likely to be available to it and how they are to be apportioned among different parts of the public sector; it has to indicate to the private sector its requirements, and learn from the private sector the latter's future capabilities. Since the two sectors do not meet in Parliament an outside meeting-place has to be arranged.

The United Kingdom missed out on the first more basic and therefore simpler phase of economic planning. It took to planning fifteen years after the end of the Second World War, precisely at the moment when planning was becoming more complicated, when prediction had to be attempted by both public and private sectors together, each taking into account the viewpoint of the other. The machinery set up for this joint exercise in prediction was modelled on the French. France had had a *Commissariat au Plan*, independent of the Government, but enjoying the confidence of the Government and operating on its periphery. In the United Kingdom there was established a National Economic Development Office (NEDO), also independent of the Government; its founder, Mr Selwyn Lloyd, attached importance to its independence and fought hard and successfully to secure it. Since what is involved is not only an exercise in prediction but also an act of diplomacy between public and private sectors, it can be contended that the exercise is likely to be better performed by somebody independent of both. Be this as it may, the Office in London, enjoying, like its counterpart in Paris, independence of Government, yet failed, unlike its counterpart, to command the confidence of Government. Its view of the feasible was seen by Government as unrealistic. And when, in October 1964, Labour assumed power, the act of prediction was taken over by the Government itself. A function, like that of the 'Three Wise Men', had been placed outside politics, only to be snatched back again.

Perhaps this was inevitable because of an initial flaw in Mr Selwyn Lloyd's concept. For alongside the NEDO, or more exactly over and above it, he also established a National Economic Development Council (NEDC). The Council was in effect the 'Parliament', the forum in which public and private sectors met. The Office was the 'civil service', supplying the forum with analyses and recommendations. The Council comprised representatives of the employer organizations, the trade unions and the Government, as well as some independent members. Throughout both Conservative and Labour administrations, the Council has been chaired by a Minister. Chairmanship by a Minister could mean that a set of predictions was not a matter for diplomacy or mediation between the public and private sectors, that it was a matter for Ministerial determination, and that consultation with representatives of managements and trade unions was nominal only. The Labour Government, having taken planning back into Government and having published its first plan in 1965, certainly incurred the charge of inadequate consultation.

The first institution set up to look at particular incomes – the National Incomes Commission – was not represented on the National Economic Development Council. Its detailed investigations were never related therefore to the wider economic background which was the Council's concern. Its basic guideline on increases in incomes was no doubt taken either from the Government or the Council, but there was no feed-back into the Council's deliberations. Mr Maudling, who succeeded Mr Selwyn Lloyd as Chancellor of the Exchequer in 1962, did indeed try, although unsuccessfully, to import into the Council's discussions a debate on prices and incomes.

Matters changed with the advent of a Labour Government in October 1964. In December of that year Mr George Brown, the Secretary of State for Economic Affairs, published the Statement of Intent on Productivity, Prices and Incomes, a good six months before he published his 1965 plan. There was no connection between the two beyond a common underlying assumption about the rate of increase in output per head, an assumption which, modest though it seemed, proved initially too optimistic. There was no attempt to utilize the instrument of a prices and incomes policy to help realize specific predictions in the plan; nor was there any attempt to place specific predictions at the service of a prices and incomes policy or to help determine a strategy for the policy. Planning and prices and incomes were kept completely separate. In this respect British planning evolved differently from its French model. In France it was the realization that planning had to be in terms of future money values not just future real quantities that drove the planners towards a prices and incomes policy. In the United Kingdom the prices and incomes policy was a separate matter. This proved to be one of the defects of the prices and incomes policy; but more of that later.

The pertinent point is that Mr George Brown succeeded where Mr Maudling had failed – into a forum initially conceived as having to do with planning, the National Economic Development Council, he introduced, and subsequently secured agreement on, the question of a prices and incomes policy. In rapid succession to the Statement of Intent there were published, in February 1965, a White Paper on the *Machinery of Prices and Incomes Policy* (Cmnd 2577) announcing the intention to establish a National Board for Prices and Incomes and, in April 1965, a further paper on the criteria by which to judge individual price and income movements entitled *Prices and Incomes Policy* (Cmnd 2639). Both carried the statement that they had been the subject of discussion by the Council and had received the endorsement of the Council. On becoming Chairman of the Board I also became, unlike the chairman of the National Incomes Commission, a member of the Council, *ex officio*.

I cannot, however, pretend that the presence of the Board's chairman on the Council thereby ensured that the work of the two bodies became integrated. The two bodies remained essentially separate. Perhaps they would always have been separate. But separation was increased by changes in the prices and incomes policy. The most fundamental change was in 1966,

when for the 'voluntary' policy started in 1965 there was substituted a policy fortified – if that is the right word – by legal
sanctions. In each of the ensuing years, 1967, 1968 and 1969, both
the sanctions and the criteria by which the Board was required
to judge individual prices and incomes were modified. But the
changes were never discussed inside the Council, nor for that
matter with the Prices and Incomes Board. The changes were
the Government's own. The only aspect of the policy discussed
in the Council was the annual review of trends in prices, productivity and incomes prepared by the Office and the publication
of which was normally sanctioned by the Council. This was a
macro-economic review, in the preparation of which the Prices
and Incomes Board played no part.

The reason why prices and incomes policy, as distinct from
prices and incomes figures, tended not to feature much in the
Council's agenda, is fairly clear. The Statement of Intent had
been in the nature of a Concordat. Each signatory of a Concordat
is dimly aware of limits to his power. The Government could not
accelerate the rate of economic growth without action by
managements and unions on prices and incomes. Managements
could not stem rising wage costs without action by Government
and unions. And unions could not stem rising prices without
action by Government and managements. Each one of the three
was dependent on the other. With the introduction in 1966 of
legislation governing prices and incomes, legislation which was
not the outcome of negotiation but of Government fiat, the
perception of inter-dependence became obscured, though the
inter-dependence was still in fact there. Legislation and changes
in legislation became privy to Government, with other 'interests'
represented in the Council being informed of the Government's
decisions. Legislation gave Government an impression of power
which it did not have. This need not necessarily have been so,
but it was so. The combination of economic policies followed from
1966 onwards gave the trade unions the impression that it was
they who were being victimized. They reacted accordingly. The
resulting pay explosion of 1970 caused managements to believe
that it was they who were being hammered. And they in their
turn lost their faith in the policy.

The Prices and Incomes Board had been the outcome of the initial Concordat. Somebody was required to help ensure that each signatory to the Concordat played his promised part – employers, trade unions, and the Government, the last both as an employer who paid wages and salaries and as a seller of goods and services for which prices were charged. This somebody could not be the National Economic Development Council, the formal source of the Concordat. Nor plainly could it be the Government, a party to the Concordat. There had to be an independent judge, expertly scrutinizing the actions of employers, unions and Government according to the criteria set down for it, criteria in the formulation of which the judging body played no role, which were in the main economic but which were also in part social. The establishment of this special kind of 'judge' was of considerable constitutional significance. Before we can fully appreciate what this statement means, we must consider in detail the operations of the Prices and Incomes Board.

Part 2

How to Run a Prices and Incomes Policy

Chapter Five

Criteria for Wages:
Incentives versus Fairness

The National Board for Prices and Incomes represented the latest stage in an evolution, an evolution in the course of which Governments drawn from the main political parties in the United Kingdom had come to recognize that to cope with the general problem of inflation and the particular problem of the Government as an employer, they had to do more than influence general quantities such as the level of total spending or the supply of money; they had to influence particular prices and incomes. For this purpose rules for judging prices and incomes or movements in these were drawn up as part of a treaty between the Government and the representative organizations of employers and trade unions. The Prices and Incomes Board was the 'judge' appointed to consider whether or not individual price or incomes decisions referred to it by the Government were in accordance with the agreed rules. The Board could only report its findings to the Government, which could then act or not act, as it thought fit.

The Board's members were drawn from both the Conservative and Labour Parties, from both management and trade unions. But whatever their origin they accepted that they should work to the rules laid down for them, in so far as these gave them clear guidance.

Let us first consider the rules or the criteria as they were intended to apply to incomes. By incomes we mean, in the main, incomes from employment – that is, weekly wages and salaries paid by the month or over some longer period of time. There is a difference between wages and salaries which can be a source of awkwardness in the running of a prices and incomes policy: some salaries are subject to annual additions or increments, reflecting seniority, whereas wages normally are not. This is, however, a difficulty of detail which need not concern us unduly. Over one half of all income from employment consists of wages. 'Wages' is therefore a convenient shorthand expression for all incomes earned in the course of employment.

The criteria consisted of two parts: first, a general rule on the size of the desirable movement in wages; second, exceptions from the general rule considered justifiable either on economic grounds or on grounds of equity. The requirements of efficiency, on the one hand, and fairness, on the other, have come to be regarded as poles apart: efficiency, so it is thought, being encouraged by the prospect of unduly high rewards and being retarded by an undue concern for fairness. The analysis of inflation given in Chapter Two has given us cause to question the desirability of an extreme contradiction between the two. In the context of inflation considerations of what is economically desirable and what is equitable are not necessarily in conflict with one another, for we have seen that at the root of inflation there lies a sense of inequity.

We should note that we are not concerned with the determination of a wage for a specific kind of labour in a vacuum; we are concerned with the movement from the existing level of wages. We need a rule indicating what this movement should be, for society left to itself will otherwise determine its own rule; a spirit of emulation or a striving after equality or a desire to maintain one's position relatively to others ensuring that nearly everybody follows somebody else's increased lead, this lead being set by a combination of power or circumstance or chance, the entire process ending up by being inflationary. Experience has shown that if the Government fixes a low standard for wage increases for its own employees in the hope of setting an example for the rest of society it will not be followed. The pay 'pause' of 1961–2 in the United Kingdom obtained in the public sector only; there is no evidence that the private sector followed suit, though the 'pause' in the public sector clearly affected the composite wage index for the entire economy. For this reason the standard has to be agreed upon with employers and trade unions operating in the private sector and to be applicable to both private and public employees.

How then shall the standard rule for wage increases be defined?

In the United Kingdom in 1965 it was done with reference to the estimated annual increase in output per head for the next five years – namely, 3 to $3\frac{1}{2}$ per cent. It was thought that in the earlier years of the half decade the annual increase in output per head would be below this figure and in the later years above it. Things did not turn out quite like this, but as a rough average of the annual increase in productivity over the next half decade the figure was not far off the mark.

Throughout the five years 1965 to 1970 the standard had various names. Up until the financial crisis of July 1966 it was called the 'norm' meaning an average; that is to say, some pay increases were to be below the standard, some above, the latter depending on whether they were reckoned as exceptions. From July 1966 until the end of 1967, that is, after the devaluation of the pound sterling, the 'norm' was put at zero and the exceptions held justifiable were extremely limited in number. While the term was the same, this change was in fact a change of definition, for, strictly speaking, a zero 'norm' should have meant that some had decreases in their pay and others increases. It is not clear that this was the intention and it certainly was not the practice. The reduction in the 'norm' from $3-3\frac{1}{2}$ per cent to zero was intended to offset increases in pay above the 'norm' which had taken place in 1965–6, so that over the half decade as a whole pay increases would still be roughly equivalent to the expected increase in productivity. The drastic action of promulgating a zero 'norm' or a 'freeze' was intended to avert a devaluation in the exchange rate of the pound. Nonetheless, the pound was devalued in November 1967. After devaluation, through 1968 and 1969, the standard increase was termed a maximum or 'ceiling', with only very limited exceptions above the 'ceiling'. The word 'ceiling' was clearly intended to convey a sense of severity, a severity needed if the benefit to the balance of payments resulting from devaluation were to be realized. For the first half of 1970 the standard became a 'range' of $2\frac{1}{2}$ to $4\frac{1}{2}$ per cent – clearly a looser term, though the figures had not greatly changed.

There was one lesson to be learnt from this changing nomenclature. Whatever the term, the figure promulgated as the 'standard' for increases in incomes turned out in practice to be a *minimum.* This fact need not surprise us. It arises from the nature of the problem – people want at least the increase which they see others enjoying. 'Norms', 'averages', 'ranges' – any dispersion of wage increases implied in these terms defies this fact of modern society. If, of the terms used between 1965 and 1970, there is one less open to objection than any other it is probably the 'maximum' or 'ceiling', with provision for limited but clearly reasoned exceptions above the 'ceiling'.

I was not party to the debate which produced the definition of the standard wage increase as being equivalent to the prospective and future rates of increase in the gross domestic output per head. I was simply instructed and could, therefore, not take exception to it. Being prospective it carried with it risks: if the rate of increase in national output per head turned out to be less than the standard, then even pay increases kept to the standard would prove to be inflationary. The Kennedy Administration in the United States had been more cautious: its 'guidepost' policy had tried to ensure that increases in incomes were equivalent to the *past* rate of increase in national output per head; pay increases were, therefore, to be based on increases in output already realized.

The basing of the standard for increases in wages on the rate of increase in the gross domestic product per head, past or prospective, is logical in that, if adhered to, it should ensure general stability in prices. But, alas, every policy starts with a heavy legacy from the past. Wages had been rising at a faster pace than that now allowed for in the new policy. Firms were reacting to previous pay increases by continuing to raise prices – we shall have to discuss this problem at greater length when we come to consider prices. Let us note now that this was one of the factors operating from the outset to undermine the policy. In the year of July 1966 to mid-1967, the period of the 'freeze', when both wages and prices were to be held roughly at their then levels, prices were not allowed to reflect past increases in costs. Wages were as a result better held. Prices were, however, allowed to reflect increases in indirect taxes. The later spectacle of prices rising on this account while wages were held stable contributed considerably to the ultimate destruction of the 'freeze'. Finally when devaluation came, the prices of imported goods rose. Devaluation implies that costs have been pushed upwards by pressures to attain living standards beyond the country's competitive power, and, unless devaluation is to be a repeated measure, these pressures must be contained. The aftermath of devaluation is thus the moment for promulgating a new standard governing wage increases; unfortunately, this above all others is the most difficult period in which to maintain such a standard, for pay will now be under the strain of rising import prices. For this reason a sudden large alteration in the rate of exchange is an instrument of doubtful efficacy in bringing a nation's living standards more into keeping with its competitive ability: this particular 'market mechanism', like others, may encounter strong social resistances. Devaluation was indeed followed by intensified wage claims. As a result, the standard for wage increases related to the rate of increase in output per head had become unrealistic. The 'norm' of $3-3\frac{1}{2}$ per cent given to the Board on its inception in 1965 was difficult enough to attain; it compared with a post-war annual rate of increase in earnings of 6 to $6\frac{1}{2}$ per cent. But the 'range' of $2\frac{1}{2}$ to $4\frac{1}{2}$ per cent given to the Board in December 1969, when earnings were increasing at the rate of about 10 per cent a year, was impossibly unrealistic.

Rising prices were not alone in undermining the 'norm'. They were aided and abetted by rising taxes. When account is taken both of rising prices and rising taxes the 'norm' for wage increases was far from being attained. Between 1964 and 1968 the annual rate of increase in the real take-home pay (that is, what pay will buy after tax) of manual workers in the United Kingdom was only 0·5 per cent; between 1968 and 1970 it was somewhat higher at 1·3 per cent.* Once this is seen the 'norm' cannot be expected to command wide assent.

We reach, then, this position: a 'norm' for wage increases related to the rate of increase in the gross domestic product per head appears economically sensible because this is roughly what the country can afford without rising prices; it also appears fair because it is a crude measure of what everybody can be regarded

* Dudley Jackson, H. A. Turner and Frank Wilkinson, *Do Trade Unions Cause Inflation?*, Cambridge University Press, 1972, p. 66.

as entitled to receive. But it can diverge too much from the situation as it has been and as it may be developing. For this reason among others the 'norm' cannot stand alone; it has to be complemented by other rules.

In the United Kingdom throughout the half decade 1965–70, the 'norm' could be exceeded in certain allowed categories of cases. The customary task of the Board was to judge whether a particular pay claim or settlement legitimately qualified as an exception. The more severe the application of the policy, the fewer were the number of exceptions allowed; and, vice versa, the less severe was the policy the more numerous were the exceptions. This fact sheds some light on the nature of the problem posed by incomes policies.

Every prices and incomes policy is marked at its inception or resumption (if it has lapsed) by doubts as to whether in fact it is enforceable. Different administrations reflect these doubts differently. Some confine themselves to vague exhortations for restraint in pay claims or aim to be educational in the sense of inculcating a more enlightened or longer-term view of self-interest. Others strike a compromise formula such as something lower by way of an increase than that represented by the settlement before. Yet others attach exceptions to a published figure or 'norm' (the case under consideration), the number of exceptions being more or less numerous. There is, thus, a scale of policies ranging from loose to tight. The history in the United Kingdom until 1970 was a movement from the looser end of the scale to the tighter, with a subsequent slight relaxation. The ultimate in tightness is for everybody to have the same percentage increase or alternatively the same absolute increase. But such tightness does not take into account the different circumstances of different groups when the policy is started. For example, on the very eve of the policy some groups may have already been promised a pay increase greater than that which the policy has in mind. Again prices will probably be rising fast, so that those receiving the standard increase in money wages may not be receiving nearly the equivalent increase in real wages, as we have just seen. Yet again, looking to the future, changes may be required in the relative incomes of different groups of people either on grounds of fairness or on grounds of efficiency – that is, to help the economy to function better. The ultimate – the same increase for everybody – cannot, therefore, be adhered to for long (six months in the United Kingdom in 1966) and exceptions there have to be. The question, then, is whether the exceptions to the standard increase will disrupt the 'norm' itself. The greater the number of exceptions the greater the threat of disruption. On the other hand, the fewer the number of exceptions permitted the greater the likelihood of a sense of grievance because little account may have been taken of this or that special case. Let us look at the experience of the Prices and Incomes Board from the point of view of trying to determine where the right balance may lie.

The exceptional categories in the United Kingdom in 1965–70 were initially four in number. They were: *

1. where the employees concerned, for example by accepting more exacting work or a major change in working practices, make a direct contribution towards increasing productivity in the particular firm or industry. Even in such cases some of the benefit should accrue to the community as a whole in the form of lower prices;

2. where it is essential in the national interest to secure a change in the distribution of manpower (or to prevent a change which would otherwise take place) and a pay increase would be both necessary and effective for this purpose;

3. where there is general recognition that existing wage and salary levels are too low to maintain a reasonable standard of living;

4. where there is widespread recognition that the pay of a certain group of workers has fallen seriously out of line with the level of remuneration for similar work and needs in the national interest to be improved. *

Of the four, Numbers 2 and 3 were scarcely ever used; Number 1 was used frequently, indeed too frequently; and Number 4 posed a dilemma which was never entirely resolved.

Let us start with Number 2: an exceptional increase judged 'necessary and effective' for an improved distribution of manpower. The adjectives 'necessary' and 'effective' both proved to

* *Prices and Incomes Policy*, April 1965, Cmnd 2639, pp. 8–9.

be difficult to interpret. For example, an early reference to the Prices and Incomes Board was a claim by London busmen for an increase in basic rates of about 6·6 per cent. The employer, the London Transport Board, considered that the claim should be met on the ground of a shortage of manpower. The measure of manpower shortage most readily adduced was the ratio of vacancies to establishment, being in March 1966 around 12–13 per cent. The 'establishment' was determined by the services scheduled. However, the relevant report of the Prices and Incomes Board said, 'There is no guarantee . . . that these services are all necessary. For a number of years the Central Bus Committee of the TGWU (Transport and General Workers' Union), opposed reductions in London Transport's services despite falling demand. Recently they have assented to the five-day week agreement which provides for scheduling services according to the staff available. When the new schedules come into operation there will therefore be substantial cuts in the establishment. Establishment figures necessarily reflect a historical pattern of services and are therefore a very uncertain measure of staff shortage.* The contention that the exceptional increase was 'necessary' because of a shortage of manpower was thus difficult to sustain.

It was also difficult in this particular instance to prove that the exceptional increase was likely to be 'effective', for past increases had been shown not to be effective. Pay increases to London busmen in 1964, following a report by a committee under the chairmanship of Professor Henry Phelps Brown,† had been intended to increase the labour force 'up to the present establishment', and the Board found that: 'The resulting advantage to the London busmen has not yet been eroded to any great extent by subsequent pay increases to other Londoners, but no permanent addition has been secured to London Transport's labour force.'‡

* NBPI, *Pay and Conditions of Busmen*, Cmnd 3012, p. 16. For a fuller account of the Board's Reports mentioned in this and the following chapter, see Joan Mitchell, *The National Board for Prices and Incomes* (Secker and Warburg, 1972), Chapter Four.

† Committee of Inquiry to Review the Pay and Conditions of Employment of the Drivers and Conductors of the London Transport Board's Road Services, appointed on 20 November 1963.

‡ NBPI, *Pay and Conditions of Busmen*, p. 17.

London busmen were not, however, a unique case. To prove that an exceptional pay increase was 'necessary' to redress a general shortage of manpower proved equally difficult elsewhere. In the case, for example, of hospital nurses there was no problem of recruitment, but there was one of retention – at specific points: '... in particular grades, in particular types of hospital, and at particular periods of the week and the day. We did not find evidence of a general shortage affecting every grade and type of hospital. Shortages were most serious in the staff nurse grade, in staffing at nights and weekends, and in psychiatric and chronic sick including geriatric hospitals.' * The remedy lay only in part in pay – a larger differential, for example, in psychiatric hospitals and an enhanced hourly rate for work at night; in part it was to be found in better organization – for example, an 'effort to increase the numbers of married women returning to nursing as part-timers, particularly in the evening.'†

To show that an exceptional pay increase would prove 'effective' meant showing that it was unlikely to be countered, and therefore frustrated, by similar pay increases elsewhere. Effectiveness in this sense could seldom, if ever, be shown. In 1965 the Midland Bank settled on an exceptional pay increase for its staff because it felt its ability to recruit to have been adversely affected by a salary increase granted by one of the largest insurance companies. In fact, 'the other clearing banks followed the Midland ... although not all to the same extent – and more insurance companies also granted increases.' ‡ The increase was thus ineffective.

What these examples suggest is that employers appear to act on the assumption that there is a labour market in the sense that wage changes play a major part in allocating labour as between one industry or occupation and another, and that this assumption leads them to general pay increases which prove not to be justified. The Board's experience in this respect would appear to confirm

* N B P I, *Pay of Nurses and Midwives in the National Health Service*, Cmnd 3585, p. 44.

† N B P I , *Pay of Nurses and Midwives in the National Health Service*, p. 46.

‡ N B P I, *Salaries of Midland Bank Staff*, Cmnd 2839, p. 13.

the findings of various empirical studies indicating that the labour market operates very imperfectly. For example, one such study concluded that '. . . redistribution [of labour] seems to be obtainable . . . largely via the (socially more acceptable) route of varying job opportunities (rather than by varying wages).'* A second suggested: '. . . changing wage differentials appear to play a very small role in inter-industry movements of labour. Industries have in general been able to expand their employment as necessary by increasing their interception of new entrants, the unemployed and employed jobseekers.'† And a third found that: 'Industries can adjust their labour supplies without changes in their relative wage position. . . There does not appear to be any significant and statistical relationship between industrial wage and employment changes.'‡

We need not infer from all this that there is no labour market at all. It is possible that a firm which pays less than a near competitor suffers, not a loss of labour, but a decline in the quality of labour retained. There is no easy means, however, of measuring the quality of labour. This modified view of the functioning of the labour market does not, therefore, help us forward.

The conclusion appears inescapable – an exception to the 'norm' on the ground that it is necessary to provide incentives for an improved distribution of manpower is better omitted, as indeed it was during the tighter phases of the policy between 1965 and 1970. Omission would not mean that a prices and incomes policy would make for a 'misallocation' of labour. Nor need it mean that the problem of distribution would be neglected. It is better attended to, however, by the elaboration of labour market policies designed to provide workers with training and retraining, information, and help to move from one place to another – that is, by policies outside a prices and incomes policy.

The other ground for an exceptional pay increase which occasioned difficulties for the Board was that of generally recog-

* Brian Reddaway, 'Wage Flexibility and the Distribution of Labour', *Lloyds Bank Review*, October 1959.
  † Pieter de Wolff, *Wages and Labour Mobility*, OECD, 1965.
  ‡ Laurence Hunter and Graham Reid, *Urban Worker Mobility*, OECD, 1968.

nized poverty – namely, exception Number 3, where there was 'a general recognition' that pay levels were 'too low to maintain a reasonable standard of living'. There were two occasions when the Board made use of it, both in relation to agricultural workers. On the first of these the Board was specifically asked to examine agricultural pay having specific regard 'to the complex aspects of the criterion'.* On the second the criterion did not, in fact, constitute an exception, and the Board had 'no option ... but to conclude that the proposed increase is outside the terms of the current White Paper, which we are obliged by statute to observe'. It added, however, that 'While, therefore, we ourselves are precluded from approving the proposed increase, we suggest that the Government would be justified in considering whether a special exception to the requirements of the White Paper ought to be made in this case.'†

What were the 'complex aspects' of the criterion which made it so difficult to interpret? One was that the standard of living of an individual wage earner was to a considerable extent determined by family responsibilities. Clearly these differed from individual to individual. The problem was akin to that encountered in determining a minimum wage. A particular figure in terms of pounds per week – and different figures are often put forward – had to be related to the estimated needs of a particular type and size of family. 'In some instances the family chosen is a couple with one dependent child and the mother not at work. But the great majority ... of adult male wage and salary earners are not the bread-winners of such a family. Nor is it possible to select any more "representative" family.'‡ The Board accordingly granted the pay increases on the ground that *average* earnings in agriculture were considerably lower than *average* earnings in other industries, even when account was taken of fringe benefits. Clearly, however, a ruling on this ground could leave an *in-*

* NBPI, *Pay of Workers in Agriculture in England and Wales*, Cmnd 3199, February 1967, p. 8.
† NBPI, *Pay of Workers in Agriculture in England and Wales*, Cmnd 3911 January 1969, pp. 9–10.
‡ NBPI, *Pay of Workers in Agriculture in England and Wales*, February 1967, p. 8.

dividual worker in another industry with a lower standard of living than an *individual* worker in agriculture.

It is possible in the light of this problem that the low pay criterion could be rewritten, certainly as far as individuals are concerned. It is now a well-recognized fact that a worker's earnings may be increased, let us say to the extent of the 'norm'; his higher earnings then carry him into a higher tax bracket, possibly increase his social security contributions and reduce, if they do not lose, his entitlement to social security benefits. In other words, his financial position, taking into account tax and changed social security payments and benefits, may be no better than before. It would be possible, therefore, to word an exception to the 'norm' on these lines: namely, where an increase equivalent to the 'norm' would, account taken of higher tax and changed social security payments and benefits, leave a worker no better off than before. Between 1965 and 1970 attention was concentrated unduly on gross earnings; the poverty associated with net earnings and the pressures to which the problems of take-home-pay give rise came fully to light only around 1970, and has been brought out more fully still in the work of H. A. Turner and Frank Wilkinson.* A criterion rewritten as suggested would still be difficult to apply to a group, but it could be applicable to individuals within a group.

A further problem encountered in applying the criterion for an exceptional increase on grounds of low pay was the difficulty, if not the impossibility, of improving the position of the low paid in relation to that of the better paid. This was certainly a pertinent consideration, for poverty, in developed economies, is relative rather than absolute. This particular difficulty was to be found in many sectors other than agriculture. Thus, in engineering it was an intention of a three-year agreement concluded in 1964 to improve the relative position of the lower paid workers in the industry. 'At the end of the three year period, however, the relative position of the lower paid . . . was much the same as it was at the beginning. . . It was also the intention of the Agreement to

* H. A. Turner and Frank Wilkinson, 'Real Net Incomes and the Wage Explosion', *New Society*, 25 February 1971, and Dudley Jackson, H. A. Turner and Frank Wilkinson, *Do Trade Unions Cause Inflation?*

move towards equal pay for women . . . Again, however, in terms of average earnings, the intention . . . was not fulfilled. The relative position of women improved only slightly and certainly less than anticipated.' * Similarly, in retail drapery, in which average earnings were below the national average, '. . . it is the habit of the trade, whenever the statutory minimum is raised, for most employers to increase the pay of all, or almost all of their employees and not only of those receiving less than the new minima.' †

Attempts by the Board to improve the relative position of the low paid proved abortive, and a 'tapering formula' which was resorted to in earlier references to provide relatively larger increases for the lowest paid had to be abandoned. Writing of this formula in its Economic Review for 1968, the T U C said: 'Unions have, often after considerable efforts to establish a viable basis on which this can be done, either tacitly decided that it was not practicable – at least in the short run – or have explicitly said that it would not be possible because of the marked effect on differentials.' ‡

The problem of the relatively low paid is of sufficient importance to merit reconsideration later in the book. Meanwhile, let us note only that the 'norm' cannot have been subverted either by exceptional pay increases designed to reallocate labour, for they were not made, or by those intended to benefit the less well off, for these latter were not clearly defined and attempts nonetheless to help them were quickly frustrated and therefore not persisted with. Other things may be said to have undermined the 'norm', but not these. Can the same be said of the other two exceptional categories?

The justification for an exception to the 'norm' most frequently resorted to by the Board, and therefore subsequently by unions and managements, was Number 1 – namely, where workers, by 'accepting more exacting work and a major change in working

* N B P I, *Pay and Conditions of Service of Engineering Workers* (*Second Report on the Engineering Industry*), Cmnd 3931, p. 28.

† N B P I, *Pay of Workers in the Retail Drapery, Outfitting and Footwear Trades*, Cmnd 3224, p. 25.

‡ Quoted i n Allan Fels, *The British Prices and Incomes Board*, Cambridge University Press, 1972, p. 131.

practices', made a 'direct contribution to increased productivity'. There were several reasons both for the presence of this exception and the use made of it. Before the Board's inception there were already the beginnings of a vogue in 'productivity bargaining'. The fashion is frequently said to have started with an agreement at the Fawley refinery of the Esso Oil Company in 1960.* Undoubtedly, however, the prices and incomes policy and the Board helped to promote the fashion further. Why?

Part of the answer is to be found in the manner in which the policy developed. The policy was initially a 'voluntary' one and there were no sanctions for breach of the Board's recommendations. Furthermore some of the early references to the Board were retrospective, relating to events that had already happened. For example, the Board was required in its early days to examine a settlement reached in the provincial printing industry for a pay increase somewhat above the 'norm', though below recent average wage increases in the country. Since there were no powers to enforce the Board's findings, an adverse recommendation might leave the settlement unaffected and the Board thus flouted. The disparity between the increase settled on and the 'norm' was not great, and it seemed prudent at that fragile stage to endorse the settlement by 'justifying' it on grounds of productivity – provided an external pressure was subsequently applied to secure the requisite increase in productivity.† In other words, the Board, like successive Governments in the evolution of incomes policy, was feeling its way and acting cautiously. Later the policy (for which the Government and not the Board was responsible) became compulsory in that sanctions could be applied to support the Board's findings. In the compulsory phase the standard was zero for the second half of 1966, without exceptions, and again zero for the first half of 1967, with the major exception that a positive increase was allowed against a major contribution to increased productivity. This contributed considerably to the further spread of the cult of 'productivity bargaining'.

* Allan Flanders, *The Fawley Productivity Agreements: A case study of management and collective bargaining*, Faber & Faber, 1964.

† NBPI, *Wages, Costs and Prices in the Printing Industry*, Cmnd 2750, pp. 21–2.

Thus the emphasis on productivity was in part a response to the difficulty of enforcement. But this is a partial explanation only. The other part is to be found in the case itself for extra pay on grounds of 'productivity' and 'productivity bargaining'. The purpose of the policy, as far as incomes were concerned, was to slow down the rate of increase in labour costs per unit of output. This aim could be achieved in one of three ways: by putting a brake on the rate of increase in pay; by accelerating the rate of increase in output or value added per head; or by a combination of the two. Since different sectors show different rates of increase in productivity, the brake on pay increases should have been applied to the fast-growing sectors; by contrast, the emphasis on increasing output per head should have been laid on the laggard sectors. In this way differences in pay increases could have been narrowed. The references to the Board did not bring out this distinction. Neither did the Board's response to the references. The Board used pressure for pay increases as a lever to secure an increase in productivity without discrimination between industrial sectors. It did so in an attempt to lay a sounder foundation in economic reason for higher pay. But in so doing it ran the risk of magnifying differences in pay increases, and thus upsetting a sense of equity, with considerable dangers for the policy as a whole, particularly in the light of the theory advanced in Chapter Two.

The range of pay references ran from electricity and gas, in which productivity was rising fast; through engineering, in parts of which it was increasing rapidly, in other parts of which it was increasing more slowly; to industrial civil servants and local authority workers, whose scope for increased output per head was limited. In nearly all of them the Board, when confronted with a claim for a pay increase above the 'norm', sought to rationalize it by reference to the productivity criterion. There were, however, two parts to the criterion: a 'direct' contribution to increased productivity through, first, the acceptance of 'more exacting work', and, second, 'a major change in working practices'. The requirement of 'more exacting work' could be met through 'incentive bonus schemes in which payment varies directly with performance' – a recommendation made for manual workers in local authorities;* or the adoption in the electricity supply industry of yardsticks measuring the differences 'from place to place and from month to month' in 'the number of yards of cable laid per man, and the number of joints completed'.† These could indeed be said to be 'direct' contributions. The adjective 'direct' was not, however, so easy to apply to 'a major change in working practices'. It is here that we enter the difficult area of 'productivity agreements'.

It is important to be clear about the meaning of the phrase 'a direct contribution towards increasing productivity'. When talking in Chapter One of increased productivity in the national sense, we meant the increase in the gross domestic product expressed as a ratio of the working force; we could, therefore, say that there was a prospective increase in productivity of, for example, 3 per cent. But this did not mean to say that it was all due to the labour force. We could also have expressed the increase in the gross domestic product as a ratio of capital employed. Equally this did not mean to say that it was all due to capital. When talking of increased productivity in relation to a firm we are faced with a similar problem. We mean an increase in output or an increase in value added, expressed as a ratio of one of the many factors which may have contributed to it – more capital, new technology, better organization, more efficient use of or cheaper raw materials, extra effort by the same number of men or a changed deployment of labour entailing the use of fewer men, etc. It is very difficult to know how much has been contributed by what or whom except in the short run, with unchanged capital and unchanged managerial techniques. For example, in the case of Dundee busmen a number of obsolescent vehicles had been retained in service because, it was alleged, of 'a restriction by the Union on the interchange of buses between routes . . . Hence, older type buses have to be maintained in service in sufficient numbers to cover the entire demands of the routes upon which they are used, and an economic use of spare vehicles is thus

* NBPI, *The Pay and Conditions of Manual Workers in Local Authorities, the National Health Service, Gas and Water Supply*, Cmnd 3230, p. 48.

† NBPI, *Pay of Electricity Supply Workers*, Cmnd 3405, p. 15.

rendered impossible.'* In this case a change in 'working practices' would have led to a saving in maintenance and capital costs, and a still photograph would have shown the increase in productivity to be the 'direct' contribution of labour. Similarly, in the case of the Railways Board it was said that, 'given agreement by the staff to the abolition of traditional demarcation lines, the work of the station and parcels porters at one London main line station could be done by a third fewer men than are now employed'.† Here again a still photograph would have shown the change to be a 'direct' contribution by labour.

Still photographs, however, seldom give a true picture. A moving film taking us both backward and forward in time could show things differently. For example, in the case of the Dundee busmen somebody must have noticed that an interchange of buses between routes would yield savings; was this 'somebody' management? And in the case of the London railway station somebody must have observed that an economy would result if station porters did parcels work and vice versa. Was it again management?

In a moving film or in a dynamic situation, '. . . a change in any component, such as output per man-hour, may be merely the *passive* resultant of changes initiated elsewhere in the network'.‡ In other words, changes can take place in the amount of capital equipment used, or in technology and organization, all of them entailing in turn changes in 'working practices'; the 'direct' contribution of labour is then difficult, if not impossible, to identify. If in these circumstances there were attributed to labour the entire fruit of new investment in capital equipment, wages for such workers would increase disproportionately as compared with wages elsewhere. Alternatively if the whole fruit were ascribed to capital, profits would rise disproportionately at the expense of both workers and consumers. The only equitable rule is to recog-

---

* N B P I, *Pay and Conditions of Busmen Employed by the Corporation of Dundee*, Cmnd 3791, p. 5.

† N B P I, *Pay and Conditions of Service of British Railways Staff*, Cmnd 2873, p. 21.

‡ B. Gold, 'Capital, Labour and Productivity in Steel: Some New Analytical and Empirical Perspectives', Working Paper No. 32–A, Research Program in Industrial Economics, Case Western University.

nize that an increase in productivity comes more often than not from a combination of sources. The greater the increase, the greater the proportion of it which should go to the consumer, lest otherwise profits and wages rise disproportionately; the smaller the increase, the greater the proportion of it which should go to the worker, lest he fall disproportionately behind others in his wage increase. The criterion set for the Board confused a 'direct' contribution by labour with changes in working practices which could be prompted by other factors. The confusion became a cloud which in time enveloped the entire policy. It was the fault of the Board that it did not disperse it.

If one industry or firm were to grant a large 'productivity-pay' increase, was this likely to affect pay elsewhere? Could the exception thus have contributed to the collapse of the policy? This is not an easy question to answer. Because of the imitative nature of the pay problem, a payment higher than the 'norm' on grounds of productivity can easily be copied without any copying of the contribution to higher output. It is clear that, without rigorous scrutiny, there could be an increasing disposition to copy the claims but not the obligations. The Board twice tried to assess whether certain 'productivity agreements' had had an inflationary effect in local labour markets.* Rightly or wrongly it concluded that they had not. True, local labour markets are not the only gauge by which to judge whether or not 'productivity agreements' had on balance an inflationary result. An individual 'productivity agreement' may leave the relevant locality almost untouched, and yet have repercussions throughout a national industry. And no study was undertaken of the effects of 'productivity agreements' on a national scale.†

Despite the possible dangers attendant on 'productivity bargaining', were there offsetting advantages? Indeed there were. On the side of labour a 'productivity agreement' required some understanding of the problems and purposes of a business organization: this was a pre-condition for the relaxation of 'restrictive

* Allan Fels, *The British Prices and Incomes Board*, p. 140.
† For a discussion of this point, see Hugh Clegg, *How to Run an Incomes Policy, and Why We Made Such a Mess of the Last One*, Heinemann, 1971, p. 140.

practices'; but the condition could not be secured without arrangements for the discussion of pay against a broader background – that is, without some degree of 'participation' by workers in activities previously regarded as the sole prerogative of management. This deeper purpose of a productivity agreement has been well expressed by H. A. Turner: 'Perhaps the most important achievement of productivity bargaining is that it is helping to undermine the iron curtain which for nearly half a century has restricted negotiations between managements and employees over a large area of British industry, setting off "managerial functions" on the one hand and "craft regulations" on the other as areas which are not subject to bargaining.'* The Industrial Revolution came to the United Kingdom and other Western countries at a time when ownership had long since been regarded as implying full rights of control. Hence capitalism as we know it. Communism shifted ownership and with it control to the State. 'An absentee capitalist control was replaced . . . by an absentee state control.'† From Communism there developed in Yugoslavia in the 1950s a new type of economic system in which firms were controlled and managed by those working in them. 'Productivity bargaining' may be described as a small and independent step in the Yugoslav direction.

In retrospect it is not my belief that the exception of productivity undermined the policy; rather, it was other events that overwhelmed both the policy and what may possibly have been achieved by way of an understanding of and arrangements for raising productivity. Be that as it may, the important questions now are: first, would it still be right, despite the dangers, to provide for an exception to any standard figure for wage increases on grounds of productivity increases? Second, if so, how could the dangers inherent in such an exception best be reduced?

The answer to the first question is that some exception to the standard on productivity grounds has to be allowed. The world

* H. A. Turner, 'Collective Bargaining and the Eclipse of Incomes Policy: Retrospect, Prospect and Possibilities', *British Journal of Industrial Relations*, July 1970, p. 207.

† Jaroslav Vanek, *The Participatory Economy*, Cornell University Press, 1971, p. 91.

of incomes shows two characteristics, each at variance with the other. On the one hand, it is governed by a strong sense of equity, a sense which translates itself into a pressure for equality, whether it be equality of pay increase, equality of absolute pay levels, or, more ambitiously, reduced inequality of return to labour and capital, and indeed reduced inequality in the stock of wealth owned. On the other hand, it is also affected by a strong belief that extra money is an incentive to extra effort; the belief has probably something to it, though it is equally probable that it is exaggerated; so long as the belief has some foundation an incomes policy has to use it and guide it, recognizing that success is to be measured, not by whether the published figure is adhered to, but by whether the resulting labour costs per unit of output are less than otherwise they would have been.

The dangers implicit in the exception can be reduced – this is the answer to the second question – and the differences in pay increases designed to promote or reward effort can be reconciled with the pressure for equality *only if the differences in wage increases arising from differences in productivity movements are not too great*. Perhaps the greatest weakness of the prices and incomes policy of 1965–70 in the United Kingdom was that it insufficiently recognized this fact. Collective bargaining in the old style – that is, a settlement on the basis of a figure which makes no reference to the interests of the consumer and which is passed on to the consumer by way of an increase in prices – has been shown, from the point of view of workers in general, to be abortive; it merely results in inflation. Collective bargaining in a newer style such as 'productivity agreements' can also prove abortive; it can give rise to a great disparity in current pay increases with unequal opportunities to increase productivity; the highest pay increases will then be copied by force of imitation with inflationary results. What matters, therefore, is not just whether a settlement appears rational or well-founded in the eyes of those who are party to it; what matters also is the effect of the settlement on others. To mitigate the inflation associated with an age of equality, the benefits deriving from a particular large increase in productivity have to be spread by price reductions among a wider circle than those immediately employed in that sector. This is one of the most important questions raised by a prices policy and will be more fully discussed in the next chapter.

The fourth and last exception to the standard was represented by those instances where there was a 'widespread recognition' that the pay of a group had fallen 'seriously out of line' with that for 'similar work'. This proved in practice to be the most difficult exception of all to apply, particularly since the Board was specifically enjoined to place less emphasis than had been customary in the past on comparability.*

It has been the general theme of this book that a widely known pay increase awarded to one group tends to be copied by other groups even though the latter may do work dissimilar from that of the former. There is, however, a particular variant to this theme. Any one group is apt, from habit which may be recent or long-standing, to compare its position with that of other specific groups. The basis of the comparison is not necessarily that of 'similar work' and may vary from case to case. For example, in the United Kingdom gas workers tend to compare their position with that of electricity workers, partly because both work in recognized public utilities and both at one time had common employers in the shape of local authorities. British university teachers, putting a claim to the Board in 1968, sought to ground it in the level of earnings of other university graduates who might have gone into business or into the Government service, and were clearly not doing 'similar work'. For roughly the decade 1960–70 British doctors had their pay determined by a review body chaired by Lord Kindersley. In the summer of 1970, when the General Election was under way, the Labour Government referred to the Board the latest Kindersley recommendations for substantial pay increases. In the heat of the Election, the Conservative Party promised, if elected, to withdraw the reference, a promise which was fulfilled when the Conservatives were returned to office. As a result, the Board's Report was never published. What the investigation showed, however, was that the Kindersley body had endeavoured to maintain doctors, as far as their levels of pay were concerned, in the same relative position to the hierarchy of

* *Prices and Incomes Standstill: Period of Severe Restraint*, November 1966, Cmnd 3150, paragraph 30.

professions as had been disclosed in a widespread survey of professional earnings more than a decade previously – a course for which it is difficult to find any economic or social justification, and which does not necessarily square with the injunction that an exceptional increase be granted only when pay has fallen seriously behind that for *similar work*.

Now the central feature of an incomes policy is that it substitutes something lower by way of a pay increase for the standard which recently prevailed. The other groups with which any one group is in the habit of comparing itself may have obtained the earlier rate of increase; to give to the latest claimant the earlier rate of increase would undermine the policy. Not to give it, on the other hand, would be to affront the claimant's sense of equity; and equity lies at the root of the incomes problem; without commanding a sense of equity no incomes policy can survive. This is the dilemma of an incomes policy and potentially its Achilles heel. The dilemma was at its most acute in the first half of 1967 – that is, the period of Severe Restraint. When incomes were 'frozen' in the summer of 1966 there clearly were in being agreements to pay this or that increase later in the year. The Government, rightly or wrongly, did not seek to abrogate these commitments; their implementation was deferred for six months. Many of them thus came into effect in the first half of 1967. This was inevitably an irritant to those whose incomes were still not allowed to be increased except in very special circumstances.

The Board tried to fight its way through this dilemma – the dilemma of not giving the old rates of pay increase while yet under pressure to compare with them – by justifying nearly every increase in excess of the standard in terms of productivity. This was a mistake – not because the productivity of some people (for example, coal miners) is more easily measurable than that of others (for example, civil servants) but because in the longer run wage increases related solely to different rates of increase in productivity will not prove socially acceptable.

The problem is that the disposition to compare both levels of pay and increases in pay tends to frustrate any attempt to lower the rate of increase in money earnings. Yet such comparisons are rooted in a quest for justice. Can the quest for justice be met in a manner which is less inflationary? The honest answer is, 'Not easily'. Nobody would quarrel with an effort to pay somewhat more to the poorly paid than to be better paid. There would, as we have seen, be a matter of drawing the line between 'poorly' and 'better' paid, and there would be the even larger matter of ensuring that the better paid did not defeat the endeavour by maintaining their 'differential'. Beyond that, the fairest answer is that the definition of 'similar work' should not be left to the group claiming an above-standard increase in pay; the task of selecting the jobs with which comparison should be made should be entrusted to an impartial body; and the comparison should be made as objectively as possible with the aid of modern job evaluation techniques: for example, the differing degrees of skill and responsibility required for a job can be assessed, appropriate weights given them, and the job in this way 'measured'.

Some countries – for example, Holland and certain socialist countries – have tried to meet the quest for justice by the establishment of national job evaluation schemes attempting to grade jobs throughout the country on a single scale. The proposal made here does not go to that length. It suggests only that when a pay increase above the 'norm' is claimed because somebody else has had it or has absolutely higher pay, the jobs should as objectively as possible be compared; the comparison can have some effect on the grievance as voiced, and conceivably on the grievance as felt. The Board used this device on only one occasion – in relation to the Armed Forces. That Report* demonstrated that an assessment of jobs across industry on the basis, for example, of the degree of skill or responsibility required was indeed feasible, and could help to bring about a new acceptance of the jobs between which comparison was legitimate. It also showed that the use of job evaluation can reveal how irrelevant many inherited distinctions now are – for example, that between 'tradesmen' and 'fighting men' – and how, as a result, the number of rungs in a hierarchy can be reduced. Money, however, has to be attached to the jobs; money would reflect in some measure an old standard of pay increases rather than a new standard. Inflation would not,

* NBPI, *Standing Reference of the Pay of the Armed Forces* (*Third Report*), Cmnd 2491.

therefore, be eliminated through a more exact comparison of jobs; but it could be mitigated by grounding the claim to 'comparability' in a more logical foundation. In sum, an exception to the standard figure on grounds of 'comparability' is unavoidable, but the comparisons have to be tightly defined, and the use of 'job evaluation' techniques can be helpful for this purpose. However, they take time to prepare; job evaluation is not of itself an answer to the problem raised at the outset of any incomes policy – comparison with what has immediately gone before. Further, on its introduction it may well necessitate a considerable jump in pay – say, 5 per cent.* It cannot, therefore, form part of a short-term policy, but in order to promote a sense of equity it is an essential part of a long-term one.

I have dealt with the exceptions to the standard which the Board was empowered to take into account. Were there any others which, with the benefit of hindsight, might have been set for it but the absence of which left the Board rather lost? There was certainly one. No guidance was given on the spacing of pay levels, or on pay 'differentials', within a hierarchical pay structure. There are indeed two kinds of pay 'differentials': differences in pay between those who otherwise think themselves alike – the problem of 'comparability' – and differences in pay between different grades or different levels of society, the differences in pay being greater or less than the differences in grade are considered to warrant. Either difference may give rise to a sense of grievance and thus prove to be a source of inflationary pressure. But whereas the Board was given some guidance on how to deal with the first grievance, it was given none on how to deal with the second. Not that the matter became important, at least as far as references before the Board were concerned, except towards the top of a hierarchy. In the case of the Armed Forces, for example, the content of a job could be compared with that of a civilian job and the appropriate pay increased inferred accordingly. When it came to the pay of higher officers, however, the techniques of job measurement were not used for drawing up a comparison with civilian jobs, and the Board's recommendations were arbitrary. In retrospect there is no substantial reason why they

* N B P I, *Job Evaluation*, Cmnd 3772, pp. 42–3.

should not have been used and the omission should one day be remedied.

The problem of pay differences at the top of a hierarchy was particularly difficult in the case of the salaries of members of nationalized boards. On the one hand, the boards themselves had conceded to officers immediately below the level of the board salaries which sometimes exceeded those of board members; such officers, therefore, had no incentive to join the boards. On the other hand, seemingly too high increases for board members could prove politically provocative. Those who contended that the Board's recommendations, made in March 1969, did indeed provoke could be right – the 'pay explosion' began some six months later. The truth probably is that differentials in a hierarchy, being a legacy from an earlier age, can be compressed without untoward effect – such as, for example, quenching the ambition to be promoted. But to what extent they can be compressed is not known. Much research is required to determine an answer to that question. The topic is too important for arbitrary decision and potentially too explosive to continue to be ignored. Like the use of job evaluation to deal with the problem of comparability, it requires an organization permanently in being so that it has time to develop the appropriate techniques.

The lessons to be derived from the Board's experience with wages are these: there is a case for a 'norm' related to the rate of increase in the national product; the more unrealistic the 'norm' the greater the pressure to complement it with exceptions. There is no case for an exception to change the distribution of manpower; there is a case for a limited exception on the ground of a manifestly 'direct' contribution to increased productivity; there is a case for an exception to the low paid, but in that event the policy has to be firm enough to prevent a rise in differentials up the social scale; finally, there is a case for an exception in the shorter term to deal with the kind of anomaly which inevitably appears at the start of a policy and in the longer term to provide more rational answers to the claims of 'comparability'.

Chapter Six

Criteria for Prices: Costs and the 'Proper' Rate of Profit

Increases of incomes may affect prices twice over: first, a particular pay settlement may directly affect a particular price; second, the settlement may affect *other* pay claims, and the total accumulation of pay settlements may affect prices in general. Studies for the United Kingdom suggest that an increase in the earnings index transmits itself to an increase in the retail price index to the extent of about 50 per cent. It was stated in Chapter Two that about 50 per cent of any increase in the retail price index is also reflected in an increase in earnings. The pressure of pay on prices is thus about equalled by the pressure of prices on pay; the effect of prices on pay then takes place in very much the same way as the effect of pay on prices; one price increase influences other prices and then the general movement in prices influences pay.

We saw in the case of wages that they are determined in part by economic, but in greater part by social, pressures; and the criteria which the Board was required to bear in mind in scrutinizing wage claims or settlements were correspondingly based in part on economic considerations, in part on considerations of equity. Likewise prices are shaped in part by economic pressures, in part by convention; some prices matter economically, others matter because of their social impact. The criteria for looking at prices need, therefore, to encompass both economic and social factors.

An increase in certain prices will have a greater propelling effect on prices in general than a movement in other prices. For example, an increase in the price of steel, just because steel enters into so many products, will have a greater effect on a price index than an increase in the price of wool. Estimates for the United States showed that an increase in the price of steel reflected itself in an increase in the wholesale price index to the extent of 40 per cent. The Prices and Incomes Board, trying to make a similar calculation for the United Kingdom in the late 1960s, concluded that an increase in the price of steel had a smaller effect on other prices than this. Nonetheless, the broad proposition must be true – some price increases give a greater push to prices in general than other prices. This would be the case in the United Kingdom for prices charged by the nationalized industries. They would be both prices that mattered for other prices and, because of their association with the Government, prices that would be regarded as a signal.

There are also, however, prices which are 'felt' socially and politically, and thus have great psychological implications for incomes. In the experience of the Board one particular price increase which had a greater effect on incomes than other price increases (and therefore, indirectly, on increases in prices in general) was higher house rents. There are few countries in which rents have not been controlled, whether for the short-term wartime reason of not provoking disproportionately large pay claims or in the longer-run attempt to provide for the less well-paid accommodation which would not otherwise be within their means. The time inevitably arrives when, in order to facilitate the supply of new housing, rents are increased, possibly to the full extent of being freed or being made roughly equivalent to what are thought to be free market levels. The effect on incomes can then be significant, particularly in a country such as the United Kingdom with a strong attachment to the autonomy of local government. If rents are raised for one local authority's housing to a greater extent than another's, possibly because one authority believes that tenants should pay rents up to the full hilt while another believes they should be helped through rates and taxes, the effect on pay may extend throughout the country. There was such a case in the Board's history and the Board dealt with it by prescribing for all local authorities, at whatever level below market rents the controlled rents might be, a uniform flat rate increase of $37\frac{1}{2}$p (7s. 6d.) a week. This recommendation carried two important implications: first, the desirability of a uniform increase across the country because of the imitativeness of wage claims; second, the desirability of a gradual approach in lifting prices which are below costs to a level where they more fully reflect costs. A jump in one go could have been too devastating in its effect on incomes. Both these implications have a significance going beyond rents.

Other important examples of price increases with disproportionate effects on incomes were those of bread and beer – not because they feature heavily in the shopping basket, but because they touch socially 'significant' aspects of consumption. The most passionate discussions within the Prices and Incomes Board concerned the price of bread and beer, one group in the Board tending to see the issues as economic, another as social. There was no occasion to talk of differences of view around the Board when dealing with wages; there were scarcely any. The differences concerned prices, for prices include profits, a subject to which we shall have to return. The price of bread was the subject of a very early report. The issue split the Board in two and the publication of a minority opinion was averted only with great effort. Late in the life of the Board, November 1969, the price of beer gave rise to a similar situation, and the Board had to be invited to address itself to the problem a second time before it reached its final answer. These were the only two occasions when the Board almost failed to agree, and it was a lesson that much more than the simple statistics of pricing were at issue.

In between the prices that mattered economically and those that mattered socially there was a large grey area. This area might cover, for example, industrial sectors in which productivity was rising fast; price increases might not appear all that significant, but they might conceal large wage increases. It might cover firms producing many products; the prices of some might be raised to the levels which it was thought the market could bear in order to subsidize other products in which markets were more competitive; profits and losses on the different products might be difficult to ascertain, because of the difficulty of allocating overhead costs between them. Yet the Board was required to have an eye to the price of a product, not to the general profits of a multi-product firm. For example, the Board found it difficult to determine the unit costs of acetate filament yarn, for chemicals and plastics were produced as part of the same process, and these 'lie outside the scope of the present reference'.*

The key to a successful prices policy lay in the choice of references from the grey area. It was easy to refer to the Board price increases that mattered socially, for they were the increases complained of by Members of Parliament. Nor was it difficult to refer price increases proposed by the nationalized industries and requiring Government approval, for the Government had to appear whiter than white. But the art of picking and choosing in the grey area was new to Government as a whole, simply because it had been accustomed to trying to influence the economy through global or macro-economic measures. The selection of price references required a strategy, complementing a strategy behind the selection of references on incomes, and drawn up in the light of the analysis set out in Chapter Two. A strategy in turn demanded detailed knowledge; Government Departments did not have this knowledge, with the one exception of the Ministry of Agriculture, which had long been accustomed to settling prices for farm produce.

The criteria set out for the Board in looking at the price references that came its way were complicated. For this reason they are given in full in the footnote.† They may, however, be simply

---

* NBPI, *Man-made Fibre Cotton Yarn Prices* (*Second Report*), Cmnd 4180, p. 12.

† *Criteria for price behaviour:*
'Enterprises will not be expected to raise their prices except in the following circumstances:

    (i) if output per employee cannot be increased sufficiently to allow wages and salaries to increase at a rate consistent with the criteria for incomes . . . without some increase in prices, and no offsetting reductions can be made in non-labour costs per unit of output or in the return sought on investment;

    (ii) if there are unavoidable increases in non-labour costs such as materials, fuel, services or marketing costs per unit of output which cannot be offset by reductions in labour or capital costs per unit of output or in the return sought on investment;

    (iii) if there are unavoidable increases in capital costs per unit of output which cannot be offset by reductions in non-capital costs per unit of output or in the return sought on investment;

    (iv) if, after every effort has been made to reduce costs, the enterprise

paraphrased: where productivity is rising at a rate slower than the prospective national average then, since this is the standard for wage increases, prices may be raised; where, however, productivity is rising at a rate faster than the national average, then, for the same reason, prices should be reduced; where other costs rise prices may be raised if no offsetting reduction can be sought in the rate of return on investment; where, on the other hand, costs fall, prices should be decreased correspondingly; finally, prices may be raised to the extent that more capital is needed for investment and they should be reduced if based on excessive market power.

The criteria were in fact an amalgam of old and new ideas. The old ideas concerned monopolies. Under existing legislation relating to monopolies the Government had a power to stabilize or reduce certain prices on a recommendation of the Monopolies Commission. The power, however, had seldom been used. A similar provision was now included in the rules which the Board was required to take into account when judging the prices of individual firms: enterprises were to reduce their prices if profits were based on excessive market power. I cannot remember a single case in the five and a half years of the Board's existence when the Board fell back on this rule. This could conceivably have been because instances qualifying under the relevant heading

----

is unable to secure the capital required to meet home and overseas demand.

Enterprises will be expected to reduce their prices in the following circumstances:

(i) if output per employee is increasing faster than the rate of increase in wages and salaries which is consistent with the criteria for incomes . . . and there are no offsetting and unavoidable increases in non-labour costs per unit of output;

(ii) if the cost of materials, fuel or services, per unit of output are falling and there are no offsetting and unavoidable increases in labour or capital costs per unit of output;

(iii) if capital costs per unit of output are falling and there are no offsetting and unavoidable increases in non-capital costs per unit of output;

(iv) if profits are based on excessive market power.'

Prices and Incomes Policy, Cmnd 2639, April 1965, p. 7.

were sent to the Monopolies Commission rather than to the Board. The likelier reason, however, was that it was difficult to pin down and punish excessive market power. Suppose market power had been acquired through efficiency; was it still to be condemned? Did efficiency give a prescriptive right to continued domination of the relevant industry? At what point did market power become 'excessive'? And did not excessive market power manifest itself sometimes in a temporary cutting of prices to exclude a potential competitor rather than in the maintenance of prices? These were troubling questions; and the fact that they were troubling explains in part why the Board did not invoke the rule.

More important and more novel than the idea of monopoly was the newer idea about the relationship between increases in productivity and price movements. We saw earlier that, as far as Sweden is concerned, one particular study showed that the sectors with productivity rising at a pace faster than the average tended to set a pattern by way of wage and salary increases which was copied by sectors in which productivity was rising more slowly; the resulting increase in wages and salaries then exceeded the general increase in productivity, with the consequence of rising prices. It was added that one other and wider study suggested a similar occurrence elsewhere. On the basis of these studies inflation would be the result of an 'excessive' general movement of costs irrespective of the level of demand; it would be caused more by the push of costs resulting from social and political forces than by the pull of the market. It followed that an incomes policy required a standard for wage increases equal to the average rate of increase in productivity.

A prices policy would then need to accord with the incomes policy. To enable workers in sectors of slowly rising productivity to get the standard wage increase, prices in those sectors would need to be raised. In areas of fast growth, on the other hand, to enable consumers to obtain the benefit of falling prices workers would need to accept something nearer the standard wage increase. And only if some prices fell could the price level in general be kept stable.

To reduce prices in areas of fast rising productivity was one of the most important prescriptions set before the Board. Insofar as rising productivity is due in the main to capital investment, the industries showing it will be capital-intensive and will tend to consist of few firms. The newer requirement that prices should be reduced where productivity is rising fastest tends, therefore, to overlay the older criterion that they should be reduced where there is excessive market power and to render it superfluous. The newer idea has in fact superseded the older. In general, however, the policy failed to reduce prices in areas of fast growing productivity. The important question to try and answer is: why?

There were several reasons for the failure, some remediable, others less easily overcome. There was, for example, the lack of detailed knowledge in the possession of the Government when making the references. Since the policy was directed against rising prices it was natural for the Government to start off by referring to the Board actual or intended price increases. This initial tendency was strengthened after the policy had become statutory in that firms were required only to notify to Government Departments intended price *increases*. A firm with fast rising productivity would not need to make large price increases; it could make do for a considerable time with only small price increases. In its General Report for 1966 the Board drew attention to the need to look not only at price increases but also at price *levels*.* Thereafter, Government Departments certainly appeared to search for references in this latter category. Yet the references were not forthcoming. It could well have been that even in firms or industries with fast rising productivity rising wages and salaries were preventing a fall in costs, and therefore prices; in that event the answer could have been a reference encompassing both pay and prices, but few such 'joint' references were made. The Board had so organized itself that it was in fact in a position to deal with both prices and wages in the same firm, sector or range of products. The White Paper establishing the Board had provided for a Prices Division and an Incomes Division, each headed by a Deputy Chairman. The Board never operated according to this proposed arrangement: the interlocking nature of prices and incomes made the separation appear unwise; the same staff and

* NBPI, *General Report, April 1965 to July 1966*, Cmnd 3087, pp. 18–19.

the same Board members had to be concerned with both. But this administrative unity was more difficult, if not impossible, to achieve within the complex of the several interested Government Departments.

The making of references by the Government demanded a preliminary study of past movements in productivity in different industrial sectors. This did not appear to have been undertaken. Nor was there evidence that it was undertaken while the policy was under way.

It is possible also that there were other more intractable difficulties in the way of reducing prices. For example, it was suggested in Chapter Two that there appears to be a habit on the part of firms to respond automatically to wage increases by raising prices. They may do this without regard to the possible adverse effect on the volume of sales and, therefore, on total revenue. Were prices to be held or even reduced, total sales revenue might be increased. In the case of London morning newspapers, the reaction of some to rising costs was uncertain, but others contended that in the light of past experience it was 'uneconomical to hold prices down at a lower level than that of competing newspapers'.* The only way of proving or disproving this kind of contention would have been to put it to the test. But to do this was to bring the Board face to face with the play of power within a representative organization of employers, a phenomenon perhaps not quite so visible as within a representative organization of trade unions, but still there. The sectors with fast-rising productivity are the most important in any national economy; they play a dominating role in such an organization as the Confederation of British Industry; a Government has to carry a CBI with it in the execution of a prices policy; the powerful sectors cannot therefore be lightly upset.

For example, the Board wrote of Courtaulds: '... in their evidence both to the Monopolies Commission and ourselves [they] show in this field of their activities [acetate filament yarn] a rate of increase in productivity considerably above the average for British Industry in general. The ... policy requires that such an above-average increase in productivity should not be reflected

* NBPI, *Costs and Revenue of National Newspapers*, Cmnd 4277, p. 23.

entirely in higher wages or higher profits but should be remitted in part to the consumer. The case for a remission to the consumer is reinforced by the fact that Courtaulds' prices and profits are protected both by a tariff and a monopoly position. It is weakened insofar as a fall in profits is expected in the current year... Nonetheless some modest reduction in price would seem indicated. Courtaulds increased the price of acetate yarn when the oil surcharge was imposed in 1967, and the Board of Trade agreed in December 1968 that the company need not reduce it to take account of the reduction in the oil surcharge which had been made up till then. We consider that Courtaulds should now adjust their prices to take account of the abolition of the remaining part of the oil surcharge.' * This suggestion was strongly resisted. The truth probably is that managements had not fully grasped that a reduction in certain wage increases requires, as a logical accompaniment, a reduction in certain prices; that only in this way is the fruit of economic growth made available to the general public; and that otherwise it is entirely appropriated by the workers and/or shareholders of certain fast-growing firms.

In the Swedish study referred to in Chapter Two, the sectors with fast-rising productivity were large exporters. A firm that exports may do so at roughly the same price as it charges on the main home market (the normal practice, for example, of IBM) or at a lower price, as is frequently the case with the United Kingdom exporters. Suppose, then, that such a firm were required, because its productivity is rising at a faster pace than the average, to reduce its price on the home market. If its export price is roughly the same as its home price, it could then become subject to pressure to reduce its price abroad too; its revenue from abroad could suffer and so, as a result, could the country's balance of payments. The pressure to reduce the price abroad has been intensified now that Britain is a member of the European Community; to enforce a price reduction at home has therefore now become still more difficult. If, on the other hand, the export price is normally lower than the home price, so that the home market is the main source of profit, the profits needed to finance

* NBPI, *Man-made Fibres and Cotton Yarn Prices* (*Second Report*), Cmnd 4180, pp. 16–17.

investment for exports are diminished if the home price is reduced and again the country's balance of payments can ultimately suffer. This was probably the main reason why the Board, despite repeated requests, never succeeded in obtaining a reference on the car industry, which on the face of it appeared a pacesetter in wages and the prices of which therefore appeared to merit investigation.

Two industries showing fast increases in productivity and the prices of which had to be considered by the Board were gas and electricity, both nationalized. The Government required of them, as of other nationalized industries, that they meet certain target rates of return on their invested funds. Because, however, of their semi-monopoly position the Board suggested a still more stringent requirement designed to reflect the increase in productivity: in the case of the gas industry, 'where a new technology is making for falling costs', there should be no increase in prices, 'even though costs arising outside itself may have increased'; in the case of the electricity industry prices should be increased 'only for unavoidable increases in costs arising from outside the industry'.* It is true that, if these requirements were not met, there is not very much that a Government could do about it, beyond possibly removing certain members of the relevant boards at the appropriate time, a technique not lightly to be resorted to. In the case of a private undertaking in comparable circumstances, there is nothing at all that a Government could do, unless it had statutory control over prices.

As a counterpart to the requirement that prices should be reduced where productivity was rising fastest it was recognized in the criteria that prices could be justifiably increased where productivity was rising more slowly than the average pace. By far the greater number of price references reaching the Board concerned a price increase, the justification commonly put forward being rising labour costs. It was inevitable in these circumstances that the Board should attempt to reduce the price increase sought by indicating ways and means by which productivity could be improved, thus offsetting increased costs. If the full extent of the price increase were to be shown to be unnecessary, the improve-

* NBPI, *Electricity and Gas Tariffs*, Cmnd 2862, p. 25.

ment in productivity had to be achievable in the short term. This requirement ruled out an improvement through new capital equipment, for this would have taken time to procure and install. It had to be shown that an improvement could be obtained through the more effective use of existing equipment – for example, by a different deployment of manpower or by a changed method of distribution as indicated by operational research. A simple illustration of the approach can be given. Soon after the publication of the Board's second report on the price of bread, a price which was increased because of a preceeding wage settlement, the unions in the baking industry submitted yet another wage claim. The Board had no alternative but to show that the claim could be met within the criteria governing pay without a further increase in the price of bread. This it succeeded in doing. It suggested that, if bakeries were to adapt the pattern of working hours more closely to the variations in the demand for bread from day to day, the same output could be produced in a shorter time; average earnings could therefore be maintained without an increase in costs, and no increase in prices would be necessary. Thus both from the side of prices and that of wages the Board found itself impelled to demonstrate how productivity could be improved.

In retrospect the policy should have concerned itself more consciously with productivity in the field of services – for example, retailing, financial services, central and local administration. The services represent a fast expanding sector which uses a great deal of labour and is therefore sensitive to rising labour costs; parts of it also affect the consumer immediately while yet showing a slow rate of growth in productivity. For example, in the first half of the sixties productivity of labour in retailing was estimated to have risen at a rate of around $1\frac{1}{4}$ per cent a year, compared with 4 per cent a year in manufacturing. If prices in the sectors in which output per head was growing fast, mainly through improved capital equipment, were difficult to reduce, why should not a studied attempt be made to raise productivity and thus mitigate price increases in the labour-intensive services? A lack of strategy in the area of fast rising productivity was compounded by an equal absence of strategy in the area of slowly rising productivity.

When rising costs were put forward as a justification for increased prices, it was sometimes found that they included not only costs which had risen in the past, but also costs which were expected to rise in the future. Thus in 1965 the bread-making firms included in cost increases wage claims which had yet to be negotiated.* The gas and electricity industries similarly reckoned in costs commitments which at that stage were 'not ascertainable'.† And in 1970 an application for an increase in tea prices appeared to be based in part on an expectation that the market price of imported tea would continue to rise, though there was 'no consensus concerning the amount of the increase'‡ and the trend in prices had for some ten years been downward. The rules set out for the Board contained nothing about future costs. The Board had therefore to make its own rule, drawing a distinction between future costs which were 'justifiable, e.g., because it is known they are going to occur, and those . . . not justifiable, e.g., because they assume a rate of cost inflation similar to that known in the past'.§

The bulk of the Board's work then in considering price increases consisted in demonstrating the extent to which past cost increases might have been better contained, or in giving reasons why future cost increases should be disallowed. This, however, was the easiest part of the exercise. The criteria allowed prices to reflect cost increases provided these could not be offset by a reduction in the 'return sought on investment'. But the White Paper did not attempt to indicate what was a 'proper' return on investment. For example, when costs had been incurred before the start of the policy (particularly labour costs above those regarded as justifiable in the policy itself), were these to be allowable in price increases or not? That is, was the customary rate of profit to be maintained? The criteria were not specific on this point. There was no clear guidance, as was given, for example, to the Canadian Prices and Incomes Commission in 1970, to the effect that costs previously incurred should not now be fully recouped and that profits should therefore be cut. The fact that inflation is a rolling problem, that events present have their origin

---

* NBPI, *Prices of Bread and Flour*, Cmnd 2760, pp. 16–17.
† NBPI, *Electricity and Gas Tariffs*, Cmnd 2862, p. 3.
‡ NBPI, *Tea Prices*, Cmnd 4456, p. 13.
§ NBPI, *Electricity and Gas Tariffs*, Cmnd 2862, p. 26.

in events past, and that any abatement of the inflationary pace by whatever means – credit squeeze, higher taxes, a prices and incomes policy – requires some disregard for earlier positions, was never fully set out. The implication of the criteria of 1965 was that the customary rate of profit should in most cases be maintained. Indeed the very maxim that prices will be stable if wages increase in line with the average rate of increase in productivity assumes an unchanged rate of profit. For if, as was shown in Chapter One, the rate of profit is reduced, wages can rise faster than the rate of increase in productivity and yet prices can remain stable. The door was thus wide open for the 'Left' wing to argue for a reduction in the rate of profit, and for the 'Right' to contend that any reduction would be dire in its consequences. How was one to find the truth between those two views?

One method, used particularly by the Board in its early days, was to compare the rate of profit of the firm or industry in question with the average rate being earned elsewhere. This was also a method used by the Monopolies Commission which had compiled a table of rates of return for different industries for the period 1961–3 and had subsequently kept it up to date. But it was a method bristling with difficulties. Different firms measure their profits net of depreciation in different ways. One may strike its profit after relating its costs to the price which may have been paid for capital equipment several years ago. Another may calculate its costs by reference to the probably higher price which would have to be paid today to buy the same capital equipment. Company A may depreciate its capital equipment – that is, write off the annual cost against profit – over a shorter period of time than Company B; thus showing higher annual costs and lower annual profits than Company B. Alternatively the same company may change its depreciation policy from one year to the next: 'In the case of ICI depreciation charges have ... risen because asset lives have been shortened; the company now considers the average life of dyestuffs and pigments plant to be about fifteen years compared with twenty years formerly.'* This meant that the company's costs had increased and its profits fallen.

* NBPI, *Synthetic Organic Dyestuffs and Organic Pigment Prices*, Cmnd 3895, p. 9.

Yet again the rate of profit differed according to whether or not 'goodwill' was included in capital. In 1968 the Typhoo tea company was acquired by Schweppes for a total consideration of £45 million, made up of £4 million for cash, £10 million for tangible assets and the balance – £31 million – for 'goodwill'. The Typhoo accounts for the year ended December 1969 showed a rate of return of 37 per cent if 'goodwill' was excluded from the capital; the rate of return dropped, however, to 9 per cent if 'goodwill' was included. The Board decided that 'goodwill' should be excluded on the ground that its concern was with 'real resources' and not with the 'extra financial burdens that may have been put on . . . companies as a result of recent mergers and takeovers'. *

It will be seen that to assess whether or not a rate of return was adequate by comparing it with an average obtainable elsewhere did not permit of any fine judgement. The Board accordingly began to move away from it. It first did so in a report on cement prices in 1967. Cement prices were determined in accordance with an arrangement approved of by the Restrictive Practices Court: 'Evidence was produced, and accepted by the Court, that whereas, under conditions of free competition, a new entrant to the industry would have required a return of 15 to 20 per cent on his equity capital, members of the [Cement Makers] Federation had been content to accept a rate of return of under 10 per cent from capital which they had invested in new works'.† Here again the comparative method had been resorted to by a body concerned with controlling monopolies or restrictive practices. The Board therefore attempted a new kind of comparison – between the cost of capital and the return expected on the investment. This was an elaboration of the criterion which allowed prices to be raised 'if . . . the enterprise is unable to secure the capital required to meet home and overseas demand'.‡ The use of this criterion required answers to at least two questions: first, what was the demand which had to be met? Second, what was the capital required to meet it?

An estimate of prospective demand was patently not easy. And

* NBPI, *Tea Prices*. Cmnd 4456, p. 13.
† NBPI, *Portland Cement Prices*, Cmnd 3381, p. 2.
‡ *Prices and Incomes Policy*, Cmnd 2639, p. 7.

the Board seldom attempted it, for the most part judging it right to accept the estimates of firms or industries. Nor would 'capital required' have had much meaning expressed as a quantity in relation to demand. What did have meaning, however, was the cost of access to capital in relation to the return expected from the manner in which the capital was invested.

The cost of capital is the average of the cost of a number of different kinds of capital: long-term borrowing at a fixed rate of interest; short-term credit facilities; and equity capital from shareholders, including profits retained in the business which might otherwise have been paid out to them as dividends. Of these three main categories of capital available to a company the cost of the first two is easily ascertained. The cost of the last – equity capital raised from shareholders or funds due to them but retained in the business – has to be estimated. It must, broadly speaking, be the yield expected by shareholders on the funds subscribed. But how does one know what shareholders expect? One turned to merchant banks. On one occasion when this was done – in the case of beer prices under investigation in 1969 – the industry had anticipated the Board's approach, and had already been in touch with the merchant bank which the Board contacted. There must be some doubt about the objectivity of the answer given by such methods.

The answers given by merchant banks about shareholders' expectations contained in any case a fatal flaw from the point of view of an organization charged with damping down inflation. We see in the next chapter that a body settling, for example, doctors' pay would make inflation move faster if it assumed that everybody else's pay was going to rise at the current speed and rested its settlement on this assumption. Similarly we have seen in this chapter that the Board, when regulating prices, would make them rise still more rapidly if, in its determinations, it assumed unknown future increases in costs. As far as any estimate of the cost of equity capital was concerned, however, it was bound to reflect some expectation of continued inflation.

Despite this and other difficulties,* however, the Board in-

* For a fuller account, see Ralph Turvey, 'Rates of Return, Pricing and the Public Interest', *Economic Journal*, September 1971.

creasingly resorted to the method of comparing the cost of capital
with the return expected on an investment. The expected return
had to be expressed in, or 'discounted' to, present-day values. If
the price of the product showed a return just exceeding the cost
of capital it could be judged to be fair; if it showed too large an
excess it was too high; if, on the other hand, the cost of capital
was not covered the price of the product could be said to be too
low. The Board used this method of judging applications for price
increases not only for cement, but also for beer and plasterboard.
It was as near to an objective method as one could get for recon-
ciling the views of the 'Right' and the 'Left' as to what constituted a 'proper' rate of profit. Not that it could always be
used. Sometimes a firm itself did not have sufficient information
to make possible an appraisal of the expected return on investment;* sometimes there was no investment project. The Board
had then to fall back on 'the accounting rate of return on capital
employed by the company'† and compare it with the average
return earned.

A complementary method of determining objectively what is a
'proper' rate of profit might be possible if more were known about
the problem as seen from the standpoint of multi-national companies. It is they, after all, who primarily decide to invest in
country A rather than in country B in the light of the return
judged to be obtainable. The Board was able to touch only on the
fringe of this enormous issue in two cases, IBM (UK) Ltd, a
subsidiary of International Business Machines Corporation of
the United States, and Mallory Batteries Limited, a subsidiary of
P. R. Mallory and Company Incorporated, also of the United
States. Both parent companies had a policy of charging uniform
prices for the products of factories which may be located in
different countries. 'Unless the prices are uniform it is difficult to
preserve the integrity of one market as against another: with
different prices products from the European factories might, for
instance, enter the USA through a third party or vice-versa with

* See NBPI, *Pay and Other Terms and Conditions of Employment in the
Fletton Brick Industry and the Prices Charges by the London Brick Company*,
Cmnd 4422, p. 17.

† loc. cit..

the result that investment decisions judged right in the long-term might be quickly undermined. By the same token uniform prices will probably mean different rates of return on the capital employed in different countries, since costs will probably differ.... In the case of Mallory's mercury batteries ... the price charged in the UK ... had remained below the price charged in export markets. It had thus been open to a wholesaler for some time to buy from Mallory at the UK domestic price and profitably undercut Mallory's higher export price in the export markets ... the devaluation of the pound made this possibility all the more apparent.'* The company thus sought an increase in the United Kingdom domestic price of 45 per cent.

IBM similarly sought an increase in the United Kingdom price because IBM prices had been increased elsewhere. The Board, however, was faced with an insoluble problem in judging the increase sought in the light of the rate of profit. '... the international character of the IBM organization makes it difficult to consider the affairs of any one national subsidiary in isolation. Without access to the parent's books, an informed judgement cannot be made about the level of prices being charged ... from the point of view of the return on capital achieved ...'†

Just as in the field of incomes a permanent body was required to study and evolve methods of job measurement, so in the field of prices a permanent body is needed to identify the nature of the problems, let alone find the answers.

We saw in the last chapter that one of the criteria for judging incomes was the distribution of manpower; and we came to the conclusion that this criterion could be dispensed with because of the imperfect way in which the labour market works. The criteria for prices contained nothing relating to the distribution of capital, though clearly the 'proper' distribution of capital is important and has been a major preoccupation of economists. How does the capital market compare with the labour market? Capital is allocated partly by managers, investing funds retained in the

* NBPI, *Increase in Prices of Mercury Hearing-Aid Batteries Manufactured by Mallory Batteries Limited,* Cmnd 3725, p. 4.

† NBPI, *Increase in Rental Charges for Equipment Hired from IBM United Kingdom Limited,* Cmnd 3699, p. 3 .

business, partly by shareholders injecting capital from outside. For managers seeking a required rate of return, profit approximates to a cost; for outside shareholders, profit remains much nearer a residue. The answer probably is that shareholders have some of the characteristics of labour, but not all. Like labour, they too have their loyalties, their roots, and are not quick to move from sector to sector. Like labour they are no doubt imitative of one another, wanting a higher proportion of profits distributed if higher distribution is the fashion, as it became in the United Kingdom from around 1950 onwards.

Unlike labour, however, they have no folk memory of being the exploited; even in the guise of pension funds they are heirs to the concept of profit as a residue; they accept that rates of profit may vary from time to time and from sector to sector. The time could possibly come when shareholders were organized, when they exerted pressure to secure a specific return on their capital and so converted profit from its present state as a residual into a cost. But that time is not yet. As of this moment different sectors show different rates of profits, these differences reflecting different relationships between costs and prices, and attracting new capital to one place rather than another. These differing movements in profit rates, not encountering, as do differing movements in pay increases, the same mass resistance, are freer to play their part in the allocation of new capital resources. The regulation of profits through prices thus raises more acutely the problem of allocation than does the regulation of pay. Did price regulation lead to any worse allocation of capital resources than would have obtained if prices had been left free?

The answer is 'No', since the capital market is confronted with exactly the same problem as a regulatory body – namely, the fact that different firms measure their profits in different ways. Present company law does not require anything remotely resembling standardized accounting practice. Capital, therefore, tends to follow profits as 'seen', without making full allowance for the intricacies of method resorted to before profit is struck. If, through price regulation there came to be promulgated a more standardized method of computing profits, this could help to bring about a more rational allocation of capital between sectors.

It could bring more enlightenment to a market which is largely blind. Regulation could lead to a less rational allocation only if price references were arbitrarily made, or if the scope of the regulatory body were too limited and its scrutiny not comprehensive enough. This was one of the mistakes of the policy of 1965–70 which would need to be recognized in any resumption of policy.

There remains one final comment to be made about the criteria for prices. An 'incomes policy' was invoked in the first instance as an adjunct to a policy of managing aggregate demand; an attempt to contract demand and so right an adverse balance of payments, had not been followed quickly enough by a reduced rate of increase in incomes. The tendency to import heavily from abroad had thus continued and an 'incomes policy' had been evolved to help solve this problem. An 'incomes policy', in short, had a short-term purpose. A short-term objective presumably also lay behind a 'prices policy' which was part of a larger 'prices and incomes policy'. The criteria for judging prices which we have discussed were, however, all long-term in nature. And they sometimes contradicted short-term policies of demand management.

For example, a Government seeks to reduce aggregate demand by raising the cost of capital. In the United Kingdom in 1965–70 prices could justifiably be increased if capital cost more. In a society with a tradition of private enterprise, firms do indeed seek to sidestep an increase in the cost of capital by raising their prices, as we saw in the case of the brewing industry, just as in a communist society enterprises seek to sidestep price control by borrowing more from the state. Under the prices policy this sidestepping by private firms was made legitimate, with the result that the policy was not moving in the same direction as the Government's policy of reducing demand. A prices policy should be used to make prices more responsive to a Government's general economic policies. Nor was the policy moving in the same direction as the incomes policy, for it was endorsing a further rise in prices, whereas the policy for incomes required a reduction in the rate of price increases.

These were not the only contradictions in the policies; nor were they intentional. Different parts of the complex of policies had been born at different times and had undergone different lengths of evolution. The policy of managing demand had been consecutively followed since the end of the Second World War; the policy for incomes had been attempted fitfully and was still embryonic; the policy for prices was entirely new, its only antecedent having been an anti-monopoly policy of a different intellectual origin. The result was a jumble, just as a photograph of society at any one moment of time will reveal a jumble, different individuals and different layers of society being at different stages in their thinking and attitudes. Any attempt to assess success or failure, or indeed proffer guidance for the future, should try and measure how much was due to jumble and how much to something more fundamental. The next chapter will be devoted to this attempt.

Chapter Seven

Contradictions in Policies

Few would blame fiscal policy for failing to contain inflation if, while the Government was, on the one hand, cutting its expenditure, it was, on the other, increasing the supply of money and thus private expenditure. People would say, rightly, that the 'mix' of policies had not been right. A prices and incomes policy similarly is not to be judged in isolation. It has to be judged, first, according to whether or not its several parts are consistent with each other; second, according to whether other policies, undertaken for reasons valid in their own context, are pulling with it or against it. These other policies may be economic, political, or social. Contradictions indeed there were, both within the policy and between the policy and other policies. These contradictions reflected in part the mixture of historical legacies, in part the current confusion and ambivalence to be found at the start of any new policy.

One example of a contradiction stemming from history was that, while arbitrators of industrial disputes were doing one thing, the Prices and Incomes Board was following a quite different course. It has long been a tradition to refer to a third party – an industrial arbitrator – wage disputes which do not seem capable of resolution by managements and workers themselves. The arbitrator enjoys the status and prestige conferred by custom, but has no rules to guide him. As a recent book puts it: 'however high-flown the reasoning which accompanies his award, he can never deviate too far from his estimate of the likely outcome if the disputants had fought the matter out for themselves'.* The Prices and Incomes Board, by contrast, was a *parvenu*; and it was required to follow the criteria described in

* Richard Hyman, *Strikes*, Fontana, 1972.

the two preceding chapters. True, there came a moment when arbitrators too were enjoined to pay regard to the criteria; but to do so was to go against habit and their interpretation of the criteria was not as rigorous as the Board's. It could scarcely be expected that the contradiction would pass unnoticed.

An instance of the ambivalence associated with the start of a new policy, and therefore with the overly cautious approach, was to be found in relation to strikes. The Government referred to the Prices and Incomes Board selected cases of claims for higher pay or notifications of intended increases in prices. Suppose a particular claim for higher pay were accompanied by, or threatened to lead to, a strike damaging to exports, undermining external confidence in the British economy and therefore carrying potential danger to the balance of payments. Was the Government to refer the claim to the Board and try and hold to the criteria at all costs? Or was it to yield to the threatened strike at the price of a breach of the rules laid down for increases in pay, but with the benefit of maintaining the flow of exports and thus averting immediate damage to the balance of payments? This was a genuine dilemma. On more than one occasion the Government yielded to the strike; for example, the Prime Minister's personal intervention in the Liverpool dock strike of 1967. The contradiction was bound to sap the credibility of the policy.

The prices and incomes policy of 1965–70 revolved closely around both the events leading up to the devaluation of the pound sterling in November 1967 and events subsequent. It was initiated on the morrow of an attempt to break through the balance of payments barrier, to maintain economic growth no matter what the short-term cost to currency reserves, in the expectation that sustained growth would improve the country's competitiveness in international trade and so eventually yield a surplus in the balance of payments in the longer term. The attempt has been associated with Mr Maudling, Chancellor of the Exchequer in the outgoing Conservative Government, but it can be equally identified with the incoming Labour administration. For nearly two years after its arrival in office in the autumn of 1964 the Labour Government was intent on avoiding 'stop-go'; it saw in prices and incomes policy the chance of maintaining expansion for a longer time than might otherwise be the case. But the machinery for regulating prices and incomes needs to be well established and functioning before it can play an effective part in maintaining stability with economic expansion.

As it was, expansion was well under way when the Declaration of Intent was promulgated in December 1964. Incomes and prices were already rising fast. It was another six months before the Prices and Incomes Board started to function. During those six months I have no doubt but that unions and managements hurried through the gates before these were supposedly to close on them. In July 1965, a month or so after the Board's first reports, there was a balance of payments crisis. A second, more severe, followed in July 1966. At this stage all prices and incomes were 'frozen' and infringements of the 'freeze' were to be penalized by fines.

Thus general economic policy had been pulling prices and incomes strongly upwards, while the prices and incomes policy itself had been inserted only late in this process, so showing the introduction of the policy to have been too dilatory in relation to the impending crises. From July 1966 onwards the combination of a more stringent prices and incomes policy with tauter fiscal measures was expected to ward off the devaluation which had long been threatening. The prices and incomes policy was from this period on accompanied not by expansion, but by deflation.

The operation of a prices and incomes policy was helped by the psychology engendered by the sense of national crisis. The 'freeze' was widely respected. This fact, however, made it vitally important that attention be paid to the psychological impact of other parts of the combination of policies. It was here that unfortunate discrepancies arose. The fiscal measures included higher indirect taxes with a consequent increase in the relevant prices; the regulator, that is, the discretionary adjustment of purchase taxes by the government, was increased by 10 per cent; the Selective Employment Tax on services was introduced, thus raising the prices of services, including distribution, thus affecting retail prices; and the bulk-supply electricity tariff was increased, without reference to the Board. Each of these measures made sense in the context of the tradition of dealing with inflation by taking purchasing power out of the economy; some of them, such as the Selective Employment Tax, may have had a legitimate long-term end. But to the citizen who saw the Government asking that all prices and incomes be frozen, it did not make sense that the Government was itself taking action to raise prices. This contradiction inevitably, if gradually, destroyed popular acceptance of the 'freeze'.

The period of 'severe restraint' which followed the 'freeze' ended less than six months before the devaluation of the pound sterling. In other words, just as the prices and incomes policy had been invoked belatedly to help maintain expansion, so also was it, in its severest phase, ended prematurely, just before the period in which it would have been most useful. As far as prices and incomes were concerned devaluation had a double effect. First, it raised the prices of imported goods both for consumption and for production, and therefore had an effect on prices in general. There was, thus, a contradiction between an inevitable happening (one can hardly call the 1967 devaluation an act of policy) and the stated goal of a prices and incomes policy. Second, to take advantage of the chance offered by devaluation of increasing exports relatively to imports and thus securing a surplus in the balance of payments, the Chancellor of the Exchequer tried to depress or 'squeeze' home demand so that resources might be available to meet the needs of exporters. To this end indirect taxes were again raised. Thus people's incomes were able to buy less, partly because of higher import prices, partly because of higher indirect taxes.

It may well be that a people will not tolerate for long any direct control of incomes. But this inference cannot necessarily be drawn from the history of the United Kingdom between 1965 and 1970. What that history shows is that at certain moments a country's competitive position economically may have so declined that it has to put up with a slower rate of increase in its living standards than other countries. Such a relative decline in living standards is effected by the devaluation of the currency. The prices and incomes policy was one means of trying to put off that event and, when the event proved inescapable, of trying to consolidate the cost advantage which it gave. But the impact of devaluation and its aftermath on living standards was drastic, as is shown by the sharp rise in the incidence of taxation in the last years of the Labour Government.

The prices and incomes policy, which had been introduced to sustain expansion, had now become identified with deflation both before and after devaluation. 'Freeze', that is, a severe form of a prices and incomes policy, had now become identified in the popular mind with 'squeeze', that is, deflation. And in common parlance the two words are often, though wrongly, used interchangeably. It could be that what is not easily tolerated is not so much a prices and incomes policy itself as the sharply reduced rate of increase in living standards implied by devaluation: the reaction to the reduced rate of increase in standards may be so strong as quickly to obliterate what cost advantage a devaluation gives. The doubtful wisdom of an abrupt and large depreciation in the rate of exchange is one of the real lessons to be drawn from the events of 1967–70.

Nor is it to be inferred from the British experience that a prices and incomes policy can be more effectively practised in a phase of economic contraction such as occurred after July 1966, rather than in one of expansion, as after 1964. The higher taxes associated with a phase of contraction diminish the real worth of people's incomes after tax: if it is the real worth of their take-home pay that people have an eye to, they may react by demanding higher gross incomes. From the point of view of their eroding effect on real net incomes there is at the end of the day no difference between higher direct taxes and higher indirect taxes. But higher indirect taxes arc reflected in higher prices visibly and immediately. They may therefore be the more counter-productive. And they were the main weapon used to contract the economy from 1966 onwards, featuring particularly after devaluation in the Budgets of 1968 and 1969. Further, a phase of contraction makes for more unemployment and for greater difficulty in absorbing those workers who may be made 'redundant' by a drive for higher productivity.

Thus both in the phase of expansion and in that of contraction there was a conflict between the prices and incomes policy and general economic policy. In the phase of expansion economic policy was pulling up both incomes and prices before the machinery for steadying the rate of growth in real incomes had been established. In the phase of contraction fiscal policy was pushing up prices and therefore affecting incomes: and this was probably done to a self-defeating extent. Until it has been shown in practice that one policy has overriding advantages over others, there has inevitably to be a careful and complementary 'mix' of policies – monetary, fiscal, prices and incomes. In any 'mix' each component has to be exercised in moderation if the others are to play an effective reinforcing role. Not once in the entire period 1965–70 can this be said to have been the case.

There was also a conflict between the prices and incomes policy and broader policy. The Government would appear to have concluded early in 1969 that a prices and incomes policy was no longer acceptable to its followers. In his Budget statement of April of that year, the Chancellor announced that the Government did not intend to renew the powers of the 1968 Prices and Incomes Act, but that the Government intended to 'implement without delay' legislation designed to reduce the frequency of strikes. The problem of strikes had become the subject of heated public debates since the publication in mid-1968 of the Donovan Commission's Report on Trade Unions and Employers' Associations. The Conservative Party had already expressed a belief that the way to deal with the question of incomes was indirectly through legislation on strikes rather than directly through an incomes policy. Those treacherous weather-vanes, the public opinion polls, appeared to confirm that this was what the public wanted. In the Budget statement of the spring of 1969 the Labour Government also declared itself a convert to the popular belief.

There clearly is a connection between strikes and changes in incomes. And there is certainly a case for complementing a policy on incomes with a (subsidiary) policy on industrial relations. The connection between the two kinds of policies is an important matter into which we shall have to go more deeply in the next chapter. The thinking in 1969, however, was not in terms of adding to existing policies but of displacing them. The Government's proposals for legislation on strikes were first made public in the form of a White Paper entitled *In Place of Strife: A Policy for Industrial Relations*. By the middle of 1969 it had become clear that the Government, having deferred to a view that a prices and incomes policy was no longer acceptable to its followers, now found that a policy on strikes was not acceptable either.* In these circumstances the resumption of a policy on prices and incomes would have been difficult. It was made more difficult by the fact that a General Election could not be all that far away. I had seen Conservative Governments give way on monetary and fiscal policies with the approach of the General Elections of 1959 and 1964. I was now to see a Labour Government give way on its prices and incomes policy, though not on its monetary and fiscal policies, in readiness for the General Election of 1970. Indeed it could be said that much of the discussion as to whether a monetary, a fiscal or a prices and incomes policy is the most effective is beside the point; what really matters in a political system in which parties compete for votes is how the reigning party thinks it can best please the public as the next election comes round. Generally speaking it considers that it can best please by expanding consumption. As a broad rule it could be said that a Government with an average life expectancy of four years spends the first two years of its tenure in seeking to master the inflation generated by its predecessor and the next two years in generating its own. The political cycle dominates and causes the economic.

In the autumn of 1969 I returned from abroad to find London grappling with a dustmen's strike. I was concerned about the general implications of this event. But I found Ministers reluctant to talk about them. The number of references sent by the Government to the Prices and Incomes Board remained low and the country was at the prelude of what was later to become the 'pay explosion' of 1970. It has now become an article of faith that this explosion was simply a delayed reaction to the prices and incomes policy; that on expiry every prices and incomes policy releases

* See the account in Peter Jenkins, *The Battle of Downing Street*, Charles Knight, 1970.

with heightened reaction all the pent-up forces of resistance. I believe this explanation is much too facile and glib. The causes of the 'pay explosion' were manifold: the harsher treatment of incomes in the public than the private sector (even though one of the purposes of a prices and incomes policy was to secure greater equality); the devaluation of the pound and consequent rise in import prices; the abortive attempt to legislate on strikes; the impact of the rising incidence of taxation and social security contributions; the normal pattern of behaviour of a popularly elected government as an election draws near; and perhaps some element of international contagion, for France had had its 'pay explosion' in 1968, Italy and Germany in the autumn of 1969, and the shock waves had begun to reach out to other countries. In sum, the prices and incomes policy and the Government's broader policies had diverged irretrievably.

I have yet to mention social policy. By 'social policy' I mean measures other than prices and incomes policy which none the less touch on the distribution of income and wealth, thus affecting the prices and incomes policy itself. Measures that lead to greater inequality of incomes aggravate the problem of inflation. This must be so if the basic problem arises from the desire to hold one's own against, and if possible catch up with, others. There may have been isolated incidents over the years 1965–70 which gave rise to the impression that higher incomes were being more favourably treated than lower. A pay award to doctors in 1966 and the Board's own report on the pay of members of nationalized boards in 1968 have both been mentioned as having had this effect. Whether events such as these did indeed exercise an inflationary influence one can never be certain, for the psychological impression matters more than the actual facts. As for the facts themselves, the tenor of policy made for lower increases in real net income at the top than at the bottom, particularly when the benefits of increases in social expenditures are taken into account. There was therefore no violent collision between social policy and the prices and incomes policy.*

While the Labour Government may fairly be said to have

* See Wilfred Beckerman (ed.), *The Labour Government's Economic Record 1964–1970*, Duckworth, 1972, Chapter Four.

temporarily laid aside the prices and incomes policy from the early part of 1969, it cannot be stated categorically that it had done so permanently, because in March 1970 it published a draft Bill to establish a Commission for Industry and Manpower, a projected amalgam of the National Board for Prices and Incomes and the Monopolies Commission.

The Bill had three features of interest. First, it tried to tackle the problem of fragmentation in wage-fixing highlighted by the execution of a prices and incomes policy. In particular it entrusted to a single body – the Commission for Industry and Manpower – the task of determining pay for public servants and employees of nationalized industries. True, some categories of public servants or near-public servants were excluded – doctors, for example. Even so the Bill represented a major step towards reducing the potential for 'leap-frogging' between them. Second, the Bill required the Commission, on a reference by a Minister, to examine pay, prices, profits and dividends of firms above a certain size and to pronounce whether or not the firm was in any of these aspects acting in a manner injurious to the public interest. By confining itself to firms above a certain size the Bill saw the problem of pay and prices as one of market power: it has been my theme that the problem is not this. Mostly it is one of an affronted sense of fairness which can manifest itself without power, although power does form part of the problem. However, administratively it may be possible to deal only with firms above a certain size. Third, the Bill enabled the Commission, again on a reference, to examine questions of industrial structure, to consider, for example, whether a structure could be so amended as to make for greater competition. There was a logic in this in that price increases reflect to some extent an industrial structure. There had also been examples of a possible collision in recommendations between the Prices and Incomes Board and the Monopolies Commission. The Board had been asked to look at the fee-charging practices of certain professions, such as solicitors and architects, while the Monopolies Commission had been asked to look at the professions in general. Granted that the Board operated at greater speed than the Commission and that it never knew how the Commission's mind might be inclining, the two bodies could have come up with different recommendations – an outcome which would have been confusing and frustrating to both. None the less, given an appropriate choice of references to the two bodies, collision could have been avoided and inclusion in the Bill of questions of industrial structure was not a feature which I regarded as of overriding importance.

The Bill was still being debated when Parliament was dissolved for the General Election of June 1970. With the victory of the Conservative Party it was not revived and so never became an Act.

The attitude of a Conservative Government towards a prices and incomes policy was heralded during the election. In the course of the campaign itself the Labour Government had referred to the Board the twelfth report of the review body chaired by Lord Kindersley on doctors' remuneration. The Conservatives announced that, if returned to office, they would withdraw the reference. A few days after the formation of the new Conservative Government I was invited to see Sir Keith Joseph, the Minister for Social Security, to be told that the reference was indeed being withdrawn. The Board's report had in fact already been completed but not yet submitted to the Government. Had submission taken place, withdrawal of the reference would not have been possible.

It can scarcely be contended that the stated intention to withdraw the reference played any part in producing the election result. But it is likely that the withdrawal of the reference had an aggravating effect on other pay claims – the Kindersley award gave doctors an increase of no less than 30 per cent. And it is quite certain that failure to publish the Board's report on the award denied the Government ammunition which would have been helpful to it in battles which it had later to fight.

The Kindersley award rested on a 'league table' of professional earnings which had first been drawn up in the late 1950s. The Kindersley Committee contended that information on professional earnings showed that the doctors had lost their place in the table. The justification put forward for the award was therefore the retention by the doctors of their 'due' place in the professional hierarchy. No firm evidence was adduced to suggest that the flow into and out of the profession as compared with other professions necessitated the retention of a traditional place. Nor was mention made of the possibility that the award to doctors might cause other professional earnings to be raised and thus be self-defeating in its objective of keeping the doctors in their relative position. Nor was any attention paid to the fact that over ten years the medical profession had changed from a fee-earning one to one approximating to that of public employees with greater long-run security and less short-term variability of income, and that a comparison with purely fee-earning professions had on that account lost much of its validity. Finally the award was based not only on a comparison with the earnings of other professionals as they had evolved over some ten years but also on a comparison with other professional earnings as they might be some two years in the future. It therefore assumed an unspecified but continuing rate of inflation. Widespread expectations of inflation produce inflation. Both because of its unsophisticated approach to the problem of comparison and because of its projection forward into the future, the proposed award was, in concept, inflationary to a high degree. And the Government's quashing of the Board's Report deprived it of a rational rebuttal of this particular set of inflationary ideas. Thus do political parties struggling for power impair their subsequent ability to exercise that power.

The human mind is such that it seldom couches a claim for more pay in terms of just wanting more. A justification is sought to express the claim within the framework of a doctrine, a principle or a concept. The claim has then to be met with a counter-doctrine. In the course of time human ingenuity will find an answer to the counter-doctrine. One task of the Prices and Incomes Board or of any similar body is to anticipate all possible answers and, if driven to it, suitably to amend the counter-doctrine. This is an important argument in favour of a permanent body, and it was a basic mistake of the new Conservative Government to ignore this perpetual inclination to justify demands in principles of general applicability.

Shortly after assuming office the new Prime Minister described the Government's view of prices and incomes. It was, Mr Heath stated, primarily the responsibility of employers and trade unions to ensure that pay settlements were not at an 'excessive' level. This view continued to be reiterated until almost two years after the election. There might have been a foundation for this view had each individual settlement been isolated in itself, having no effect on other settlements and therefore on the balance of the economy. Once, however, it is admitted that any one settlement carries implications for all other settlements, and therefore for the whole economy, the contention that it is the responsibility of individual employers and individual unions to settle 'reasonably' can no longer be sustained. The Government gave no guidance in principle for settlements in general and therefore none for any individual settlement. Nor was there anybody to interpret principle or to state counter-arguments to claims for increased wages and prices.

In November 1970, it was announced that the Prices and Incomes Board would be abolished. The actual demise took place in March 1971. In its place there arose a number of institutions, some permanent, some transient, and a backward step was taken into fragmentation. In place of the Prices and Incomes Board there was set up an Office of Manpower Economics. The Office was designed to undertake research, assist and act as a secretariat for three permanent review bodies for different categories of public servants and such *ad hoc* bodies as the Government might establish. The three permanent review bodies covered the armed forces; the civil service; Members of Parliament and Ministers, judges, and doctors. There was to be a link between the three bodies in so far as they were served by a common secretariat and some members were to be common to all three. But this was a far less effective link than had been envisaged under the Labour Government's scheme for a Commission for Industry and Manpower. A consistent approach could have been ensured only if there had been a common chairman and a common set of agreed principles upon which to work. There was neither. And the fact that there were three review bodies, all the members of which were part-time, meant that they set about their tasks in the manner characteristic of British committees of enquiry before the Prices and Incomes Board: that is to say, by the interrogation of the parties by the review bodies themselves rather than by reliance on staff field work ranging beyond the particular and sectional interests involved. Thus the substitutes for the Prices and Incomes Board demonstrate a failure to understand the basic problem of prices and incomes: the balance between the two affects the relative distribution of the national income between capital and labour, so making it essential for an integrated policy to be formulated and implemented.

As far as *ad hoc* committees were concerned two notable ones were set up by the Government in the early part of 1971. Both concerned employees in the public sector. The first, chaired by Sir Jack Scamp, dealt with a pay claim by industrial civil servants. In making its award it was obviously not guided by any economic principle and the resulting figure was considerably higher than the Government had wished. In the case of the second, chaired by Lord Wilberforce and relating to a pay claim by workers in the electricity supply industry, the Government tried to safeguard the position by stipulating that regard be paid to the 'public interest'. The public interest as a concept was not defined, though Treasury officials in evidence to the committee sought to define the country's economic requirements. Officials are, however, the servants of Ministers, and we have seen that Ministers, while able sometimes genuinely to express a view of the public interest, are also led on occasion to express a party interest. *In a democracy the public interest is not something simply to be enunciated by a government acting of its own accord.* Especially with regard to prices and incomes, 'the public interest' can emerge only from a continuing dialogue between the Government, trade unions and enterprises.

In so far as the new Government had a philosophy about prices and incomes it was that, if the Government set an example in the public sphere, the private sphere would automatically follow. This indeed had been the philosophy of another Conservative Administration some ten years earlier; and the private sphere had not automatically followed. It is true that in a reasonably disciplined country citizens will follow a Government's lead. But this becomes less and less likely as authority falls more and more under question. What is more, the public sector is, to use the expression of Chapter Two, a 'sheltered' sector; it is the private sector which is the more likely to show a fast rate of increase in productivity; the private sector, therefore, can be the pace-setter. The Government's policy for the public sector may be summarized in the formula 'N minus 1' – that is, each settlement in the public sector was required to be one percentage point less than the previous settlement of N per cent. We have seen that claims for higher pay are very much influenced by previous events; that the past cannot be cavalierly ignored and that some deference at least has to be paid to custom.

The Government's formula implied that injustice would be inflicted on some parts of the public sector as against others. By its nature, therefore, such a policy would be unlikely to stand the strain. And, to make matters even worse, in the first half of 1972 the Government failed to assert its lead in two major publicly owned industries – coal and the railways. It failed because, although it said it was resisting claims which were 'excessive' and 'unreasonable', it entirely omitted to justify its resistance by any appeal to a sense of fairness or to the relevant statistical facts. And with these failures its own particular prescription for a prices and incomes policy – 'but let the Government hold firm, and others will follow' – collapsed irretrievably.

Nor did the new Government fare any better than its Labour predecessor in developing policies other than for prices and incomes which would be favourable to the containment of inflation. They may be examined under the three heads used earlier – fiscal, political and social.

The Conservative Government inherited a situation in which, while output was well below potential capacity, prices and incomes were rising fast; it hesitated in these circumstances to expand output, lest by so doing it should aggravate the rise in prices and incomes. The increase in unemployment resulting from this initial hesitancy then led to a policy of reducing taxes, a course to which the high yield of taxation would have led it anyway. The reduction took place more in direct taxes than in indirect taxes, and more in direct taxes on higher incomes than on lower incomes – partly from a rationalisation that lower direct taxes on higher incomes might constitute an incentive to higher productivity. In addition entry into the European Economic Community implied a relative increase in indirect taxes – through, for example, the Value Added Tax. For the wage-earner there was, therefore, a prospective increase in indirect taxes and hence prices. It is difficult to believe that this prospect did not to some extent affect pay claims. In sum, fiscal policy was most unfavourable to any containment of pay demands.

When it came to broader issues the Conservative Government picked up where the Labour Government left off. It believed that the answer to inflation lay, not in legislation on prices and incomes, but in legislation dealing with strikes. The logic behind this belief is that legislation on strikes, as a counterpart to legislation on monopolies, could help markets function more as they are deemed to have functioned in the nineteenth century. We have already seen that there is no theoretical or historical justification for this view. Against strong trade-union opposition the Conservative Administration placed on the statute book legislation to regulate strikes, legislation based largely on American legislation of some decades earlier, when the problem of cost inflation had yet to be discovered. Whatever the merits or demerits of that legislation the result was, at the minimum, to defer any dialogue on incomes between Government and trade unions. Just as the proposals for anti-strike legislation had ruled out for the Labour Government any early resumption of an incomes policy, so in the case of the Conservative Government did actual legislation retard the start of such a policy. The Conservatives had set their eyes on the long-term problem of industrial relations and ignored the short-term problem of inflation; by so doing they had aggravated the short-term and it is from the short-term that the long-term grows. This was made manifest in the autumn of 1972.

As for social policy the Conservatives had come to office with a critical eye on the way in which rates and taxes are levied to pay for a uniform system of welfare assistance regardless of means. For the uniform system they therefore substituted a selective system of giving assistance only where it was judged to be needed, such as milk at schools only for those children whose parents were unable to afford it. The new system must have meant a reduction in the real incomes at the command of many wage-earners after tax; in so far as wage-earners and trade union officials are concerned with their real net disposable incomes after taxes and benefits, the pressure for higher gross pay must have been thereby accentuated. True, the Government took an offsetting measure in the early part of 1972 by lifting the level at which gross incomes began to attract tax. But this relief was quickly nullified by the introduction shortly after of a more selective system of subsidized rents, with rent increases far steeper than the Prices and Incomes Board had thought prudent way back in 1968.

All in all, Conservative policies were far from being calculated to mitigate pay claims; on the contrary, by appearing to be directed against trade unions in particular they may well have served to aggravate them. The Conservatives received, however, an unexpected source of help in the form of voluntary price restraint by the Confederation of British Industry. By the morrow of the General Election of June 1970 the Confederation no longer wished to continue with a prices and incomes policy. With the coming of the election it had seen the policy on incomes relaxed, while that on prices had to some extent been continued. Profits accordingly were under pressure, and the Confederation made a dash for freedom. A year later it found that freedom had availed it little. The economy remained depressed, largely because the presence of inflation and the fear of worse inflation to come made the Government hesitant to expand. Industry then changed policy; it chose to help itself by helping to embolden the Government.

The Confederation of British Industry requested, and obtained a favourable response to the request, its 200 largest member firms to limit their prices increases for the next 12 months to 5 per cent. This act undoubtedly had a moderating effect on the rate of increase in prices. It duly brought in its train bolder expansionary measures by the Government than the latter might otherwise have embarked on. But by the end of the year's price restraint, mid-1972, little significant expansion in the economy had yet materialized; no great increase had taken place in gross profits; and there seemed little willingness on the part of most

trade unions to resume a policy on incomes. T⸍⸍
legislation to regulate strikes was still too fres⸍
   As this chapter was being written – in th⸍
the Government itself had undergone a c⸍
that, while expanding the economy, it h⸍
inflation and might conceivably be runnir⸍
it, it proposed to managements and tradᴄ ⸍⸍
the Government to seek to attain a certain rate oɪ ᴄᴄ⸍
growth; management to limit price increases to X per cent;
workers to limit wage increases to Y pounds sterling a week.
After two years in office it had returned willy-nilly to the point
at which Labour had begun its exercise of power in 1964. Why,
having successfully placed on the statute book a piece of legislation on industrial relations, did a Conservative Government
then have to gybe and sail on a course it had previously de-
nounced – a prices and incomes policy? The answer is that
industrial relations and prices and incomes cannot be treated
as separate and divorced problems.

Chapter Eight

Prices, Incomes and Industrial Relations

The problem of inflation is closely linked with that of industrial relations. The Industrial Revolution gave rise to two classes – entrepreneurs, investing their capital and making and selling their products, more often than not in competition with others; and workers, bargaining with the entrepreneurs, initially individually and later through organized groups, for their wages. Rightly or wrongly, the two classes saw their interests as being opposed, the opposition often giving rise to conflict expressed either by way of strikes, in which workers denied to entre_ preneurs their labour, or lock-outs, in which entrepreneurs denied workers their need to work. The conflict could take place within an enterprise, an industry, and on rare occasions, at any rate as far as strikes were concerned, on a national scale – that is, all workers in practically all industries came out on strike. The study of this conflict has come to be labelled Industrial Relations.

Now Industrial Relations are essentially concerned with the same problem as a prices and incomes policy – namely, how the gross domestic product (or national income) shall be apportioned among those with claims on it. True, there may be other important problems in industrial relations which do not feature in prices and incomes – for example, the right of an employer to dismiss a worker. Such problems as these are often facets of the larger issue – how the firm's revenue shall be apportioned; an issue which in turn takes us deep into the heart of social politics – who shall control the enterprises? Leaving on one side for the moment the question of control, let us note that there are two basic differences between the issues of industrial relations as mirrored, for example, in Government Departments such as the Department of Employment and the issue of prices and incomes. First, industrial relations sees only two claims on the product: labour and capital; prices and incomes, on the other hand, sees three: labour, capital (which for this purpose may be taken to include management) and the consumer. Second, industrial relations, again as practised by the relevant Government Departments, sees the State merely as a referee: it is there to keep the peace between the two main contestants for the product; prices and incomes, on the other hand, sees the State in a more interventionist role: to admit the poorer to a larger share of the product and to safeguard the consumer who is by-passed in the process of collective bargaining between capital and labour.

The idea of the State as a referee is symbolized in the United Kingdom by the presence in the Department of Employment of a conciliation service comprising some sixty officials. They are there to help when the two sets of bargainers are unable of their own accord to reach a bargain. Their purpose is to find the middle ground on which both capital and labour can meet, shake hands, and, momentarily at any rate, reach agreement.

It is to be noted that the introduction of conciliation, mediation and arbitration was, in its day, bitterly contested and took several decades to effect in the United Kingdom, from roughly 1860 onwards. Conciliation ultimately implied that the wage bargain was struck with the help of somebody not closely connected with the industry. Two quotations should suffice to convey both the nature and the strength of feeling of the opposition. The first is Preston textile employers in 1854: mediation, they said, was 'a principle alike subversive of the rights of the working man in the disposal of his labour, and of the rights of the master in the employment of his capital'. And in 1897 an employer avowed that to accept a Board of Trade mediator would 'establish a precedent for outside interference with the management of my private affairs'.* In 1972 there can scarcely be a firm or trade union which does not accept, as a desirable feature of industrial life, the intervention implied in conciliation.

* V. L. Allen, *The Sociology of Industrial Relations*, Longman, 1971, pp. 70–71.

Some countries – notably the United States, Canada, and Australia – long ago introduced legislation to regulate the conflict between capital and labour. The primary purpose of such legislation was to strengthen the negotiating position of trade unions. Despite the spirit of individualism which pervaded the nineteenth and the first half of the twentieth centuries it was recognized that an individual worker was in a weak bargaining position *vis-à-vis* an individual employer. To remedy this weakness workers had to be allowed to act in concert. Thus in the United States the National Labour Relations Act of 1935 conferred on employees the legal right 'to bargain collectively through representatives of their own choosing'. From the right of collective bargaining there followed the right ultimately to resort to the strike as a weapon of last resort. Not that the right to strike was unlimited. It was seen that a strike could confront a community with a situation of 'emergency'. The freedom to strike was therefore restricted in certain cases – for example, on the part of Government officials, the police, the soldiery. Legislation regulating the conflict between capital and labour in the sense of recognizing the right to strike was mostly introduced when organized groups of workers were in a relatively weak bargaining position – in the United States in the depths of a depression. For this reason the legislation was acceptable to workers. Only in one case was such legislation also concerned with a national wage policy. That country was Australia, which attempted to enforce the concept of a living wage. Clearly, however, the Australian legislation was not concerned with the consumer: it was designed to give added protection to labour.

In the United Kingdom the development of trade unions and of the right to strike did not, as elsewhere, take place by way of positive legislation – there is, for example, no written constitutional right to strike as there is in France and Italy. It took place rather by way of negative legislation – that is, legislation which gave workers immunity from the penalties which would otherwise have attended their working in concert. This 'freeing' or 'releasing' legislation has carried with it considerable implications for the psychology of British trade unions in the years following the Second World War. For the post-war period has seen an attempt to narrow somewhat the freedom won over the previous century or so. A premonition of what was to come is to be seen in the Taft-Hartley Act passed in the United States in 1947. As against the earlier National Labor Relations Act of 1935, which listed as 'unfair labor practices' various kinds of encroachment by employers on the freedom of their employees to act collectively, the later statute added a corresponding catalogue of 'unfair labor practices' which could be committed by trade unions.* The Taft-Hartley Act had its sequel in the United Kingdom when the Labour Government in 1969 and then the Conservative Government in 1971 attempted a restriction on the right to strike as previously known. The attempt came at a moment when the trade unions had grown enormously in power, after a quarter of a century of full employment, and when the problem of industrial relations had become submerged in the larger problem of inflation. Whatever the issue of a conflict between managements and unions within an undertaking or an industry – the problem of industrial relations – that issue can have considerable implications outside the undertaking or industry in question – the problem of inflation. The lesser and more parochial issue had thus given place to the greater national issue, though few appear to have been aware of it.

The Donovan Commission, reporting in 1968 on trade unions and employers' associations, appeared almost unaware of it; only one chapter in the entire report was devoted to inflation. The Labour Government of 1966–70, having attempted a prices and incomes policy, had by 1969 come round in favour of an alternative solution to the problem of inflation through the legal regulation of strikes. The Conservative Government of 1970 started from the assumption that the legal regulation of industrial relations was a preferable, and perhaps the only effective, answer to inflation. Both were resting their respective policies on the premise that all that was required was to tilt the *general* bargaining balance back towards managements and away from workers. Neither had come round to the view expressed in Chapter Two, namely, that what matters is the outcome in a *specific* case, for it is this which can influence the *general* balance. Both,

* Otto Kahn-Freund, *Labour and the Law*, Stevens, 1972, pp. 173–4.

therefore, ignored the problem diagnosed in this book as wage leadership. We shall give reasons in a moment why even in general terms the balance cannot be entirely tilted back. Insofar as it cannot, we are face to face with the newer problem of a third participant to the negotiations – the consumer. It was the neglect of the later and larger problem of inflation in favour of the lesser and earlier one of industrial relations that finally compelled the Conservative Government to retreat to a 'prices and incomes' policy, and to do so only shortly after the Industrial Relations Act had been placed on the statute book, thus clearly showing the fallacy of the argument that wages were the only important factor in inflation, and that, therefore, inflation could be controlled by attacking the trade unions.

Where a country faced with inflation does not already have legislation expressly restricting strike action the introduction of such legislation is fraught with danger, for it may carry with it all the appearance of being anti-union and anti-strike; it may then jeopardize any attempt to secure the participation of the trade unions in any form of social compact designed to fight inflation. This turned out to be the case in the United Kingdom in 1972. Where, on the other hand, a country has recently introduced, or alternatively has for some time had in being, legislation concerning industrial relations, that legislation will probably require amendment so that it may at least be reconciled with any rules or legislation concerning incomes. We saw how in the United Kingdom between 1965 and 1970 the Government hopped uneasily from one foot to the other, on some occasions standing firmly for the incomes policy, on others bending or overlooking the policy so as to mitigate the short-term damage of a strike to the balance of payments. A consistency of attitude towards, and therefore legislation on, industrial relations and prices and incomes is essential.

Ideally any legislation on industrial relations should try and deal with the basic causes of strikes about which, alas, we know too little. They may express a revolt against the sheer monotony of the machine. They may go further and reflect a resentment against the 'autocracy' of industry as contrasted with the 'democracy' of politics, against the fact that, whereas a man may choose who governs him politically, he has no say in who directs his working life. They may even imply a conscious attempt to impose a new social organization, where decisions are made by men actually doing the work, as against an old organization in which decisions are invariably made elsewhere.* They may in appearance have to do with claims for money, in reality with something different; or for that matter, vice-versa. These problems for the moment lie beyond the boundaries of legislation.

Legislation on industrial relations deals perforce with the problems we understand, and of those the most important is the fact that many strikes are patently concerned with pay. Any new legislation or any amendment of old legislation designed to shift the balance of bargaining over pay has inevitably now to defer to the legacy of the nineteenth century, even though the immediate consequence may be an acceleration of inflation. A fundamental requirement of any such legislation nowadays on industrial relations is that it should embody a right to recognition for trade unions – a provision contained indeed in the United Kingdom's Industrial Relations Act of 1971. A recent feature of trade unionism has been its extension up the social scale. A possible cause of this extension has been the desire of teachers, bank clerks, and other 'white collar' workers, to maintain the distance in pay which they imagine obtained or ought to obtain between them and 'blue collar' workers. Be this as it may, a certain consequence of the Industrial Relations Act of 1971 must be to accelerate the spread of 'white collar' trade unionism. The net effect of this could be, in turn, inflationary. A further requirement of any new legislation on industrial relations is that it should recognize in its guiding principles the right to strike. As stated earlier, this right is now written into the French and Italian Constitutions. It is also contained in the European Social Charter and the European Convention on Human Rights to which the United Kingdom is a party. It is, however, omitted from the Industrial Relations Act. Its inclusion would seem a prerequisite of any fruitful talks between the Government and trade unions on the containment of inflation.

* R. Williams, 'The Meaning of Work' in R. Fraser (ed.), *Work: Twenty Personal Accounts*, Penguin, 1968, pp. 280–98.

A corollary of the right to recognition is the right of registration with an appropriate authority – in the United Kingdom, with the Chief Registrar of Trade Unions and Employers' Associations. Any organisation clearly representing a group of workers should be allowed automatically as such to register, provided the elementary standards required of charities are complied with. Various sections of the United Kingdom's Industrial Relations Act of 1971 have, however, appeared to make registration less than automatic and as a result most unions did not register. Failure to register was probably not envisaged, but in the event reflected the disruptive implications of the Act.

Legislation on industrial relations seeks to deal amongst other things with the problem of the individual versus the group. An economist, viewing industrial relations as concerned with a relationship between buyers and sellers, would regard trade unions as a monopoly; his bias, therefore, would be towards giving priority to the freedom of the individual – he would, for example, be opposed to the 'closed shop', the essential feature of which is that every member of the relevant group of employees should belong to the appropriate trade union. It is this bias which is reflected in the Industrial Relations Act of 1971. From a different viewpoint, on the other hand, the relationship between managers and workers is one between governors and governed; 'government' would function the better were it easier to transmit views between governors and governed; this would scarcely be possible unless the latter were represented through a trade union. On this ground, priority should be given to the maintenance of the collective authority of the trade union. This is surely the more constructive approach.* The Industrial Relations Act of 1971, in taking the individualist approach, pitted the law against current practice. This could prove to be an unfortunate irritant in relations between the Government and trade unions. Consistency with a policy to contain inflation would suggest that the irritant be withdrawn.

American legislation on industrial relations in the shape of the Taft-Hartley Act of 1947 requires that in an emergency situation

* For a discussion of this problem, see Tony Lane and Kenneth Roberts, *Strike at Pilkingtons*, Fontana, 1971.

there be a ballot of workers either to secure a settlement without a strike or to end a strike – the employer's last offer, that is, has to be put to the ballot. And the Industrial Relations Act of 1971 follows the American model. The use of a ballot rests on the assumption that the members of an organized group of workers are more reasonable or less intransigent than its leaders. Its rationale is an extension of the idea that the individual matters more than the group. In no known case in history, however, have members of a trade union been known to disown their leaders. The solidarity of workers is a fact of life which attachment to the individualist tradition of the nineteenth century overlooks. It springs to the eye, however, once a trade union is seen as a political movement, as described in Chapter Two. There may well be a case for different devices – for example, an injunction to defer a strike for a certain time so as to mobilize public opinion in favour of a settlement. There is, however, no practical case for attempting to defer or end a strike through a ballot. And persistence in the attempt may well aggravate the inflationary character of a particular wage settlement. Events in the United Kingdom in 1972, when railway workers supported their trade union leaders in a ballot sought by the Government to end a railway strike, merely confirmed what history had already shown. Harmony between a policy on industrial relations and a policy against inflation would thus indicate that the requirement of a ballot be removed.

The Industrial Relations Act of 1971 is also concerned with the degree of responsibility to be placed upon trade unions for the actions of shop stewards and other lay officials. It may be true of the United Kingdom that a gulf has opened up between the leaders of a union and sub-leaders, such as shop stewards, the former knowing little of what the latter are doing. There is, therefore, a case for trying to make the main union leader accountable for actions undertaken in the name of the union. Often, however, this is not practicable. A trade union is not a hierarchical organization like a firm, in which sub-leaders are invariably appointed from above. It is a democratic organization in the sense that sub-leaders are elected from below. A realistic attitude towards industrial relations must therefore take note of these two different sets of cases: the first, in which the trade union leader can indeed exercise influence over his followers, and the second in which sub-leaders elected from below and depending for their authority from below are unable to take note of authority above. The inevitability of the law, its inability to exercise discretionary choice, makes it difficult for it to distinguish between the two cases. The Industrial Relations Act of 1971 places the main legal responsibility for the acts of sub-leaders on the trade union. This means that the central trade union leadership has to issue orders clashing with the expressions of democracy from below. This is unrealistic. The most that can be expected of trade union leaders is that they expressly dissociate themselves from industrial action undertaken from below. Without a more flexible approach of this kind the result could be the expression of workers' grievances in less organized and therefore less manageable forms. This would hardly be conducive to the containment of inflation.

Finally, legislation on industrial relations inevitably has to deal with the role of a Government in declaring that a strike faces the country with a state of 'emergency' and thus enables it, should this prove necessary, to use troops to help break the strike. The definition of an 'emergency' has undergone a great change over the last fifty years. According to the Emergency Powers Act of the United Kingdom in 1920 an 'emergency' constituted 'events of such a nature as to be calculated . . . to deprive the community . . . of the essentials of life'. The definition of 'emergency' contained in the American Taft-Hartley Act of 1947 was not vastly different. It was a 'threatened or actual strike or lockout' which could 'imperil the national health or safety'. The United Kingdom Industrial Relations Act of 1971, however, added to these earlier definitions of 'emergency' a much wider dimension – namely, 'an interruption in the supply of goods or in the provision of services of such a nature, or on such a scale, as to be likely to be gravely injurious to the national economy'. It is reasonably clear that a widening of the definition of an 'emergency' had its origin in the fact that a strike – for example, of seamen – might have adverse effects on the balance of payments or alternatively might have indirect adverse effects because of the inferences which could be drawn by other unions. Whether the widening should have been in this particular form is perhaps another matter.

An extension of the definition of an 'emergency' to take account of the imitativeness of wage behaviour and therefore of inflation had certainly become inescapable. What is more questionable is the discretionary power claimed by a Government should events conform with the enlarged definition. We have seen that legislation on prices and incomes in the United Kingdom between 1965 and 1970 gave the Government discretion to refer or not to refer a case to the Prices and Incomes Board. The Labour Government's White Paper entitled *In Place of Strife* similarly proposed that the Government have a discretionary power to require a ballot before an *official* strike which 'would involve a serious threat to the economy or public interest'. In the case of *unofficial* strikes – that is, strikes not authorized by the trade union leadership – the Government would have 'a discretionary reserve power to secure a conciliation pause' or a pause for reflection. The Conservative Government's Industrial Relations Act of 1971 in its turn gave the Government discretion to apply to the newly constituted Industrial Relations Court for a 'cooling-off' period of a maximum of sixty days if it thought that this would be conducive to a settlement of a dispute which could be 'gravely injurious to the national economy'. On the question whether or not a 'cooling-off' period would lead to a settlement the Court is not able to challenge the Government's opinion. Thus under Administrations of different political colour and in two quite different contexts – prices and incomes, strikes – the central Government took unto itself considerable discretionary freedom. Indeed the Industrial Relations Act of 1971 enhanced the position of both the Executive and the Judiciary *vis-à-vis* that of Parliament. Under the Emergency Powers Acts of 1920 and 1964 a Government could declare an emergency only on laying before Parliament orders and regulations which could be debated. Under the Act of 1971, however, a decision by the relevant Minister to apply to the National Industrial Relations Court for a 'cooling-off' period placed the matter *sub judice* and thus not open to Parliamentary debate. Furthermore, in requiring the

Industrial Relations Court to 'rubber-stamp' the Minister's view that a 'cooling-off' period was desirable, the Act went far towards making the Court an arm of Government, not part of the independent arm of the Judiciary.

The discretionary power of Government is also to be found in British legislation with regard to acquisitions and monopolies. The Department for Trade and Industry has discretion to refer or not to refer to the Monopolies Commission a proposed acquisition or a suspected situation of monopoly. The Department is required to list annually the complaints it has received on grounds of monopoly. It has not, however, been under any obligation to set out the reasons why it has not referred some cases while it has referred others of an apparently similar nature.

We thus find that over time the problem of industrial relations has become merged with the larger problem of inflation; that in the United Kingdom at any rate Governments, in seeking to cope with either, have ended by aggravating the other; and that in delineating the Government's role in relation to both problems they have chosen for themselves a discretionary power, a right to pick and choose. Before assessing the wisdom of leaving to Government a discretionary role, and before seeking a unified approach to the problems of industrial relations and inflation, we need first to look at prices and incomes policies in countries other than the United Kingdom.

Chapter Nine

Prices and Incomes Policies in Other Countries

It was stated in Chapter One that the problem of inflation is now almost universal, and that its universality may be due in part to the growth in international trade, in part to the sharing, particularly by countries of a Western European type, of common social ideals, both factors serving to transmit inflation from one country to another. Countries faced with a common problem tend to resort to common remedies, though the details of the remedies will vary according to the history and the institution of the country. There are few countries that have not been forced to adopt, in some form or other, a prices and incomes policy. This is not the place for a comprehensive review of such policies. It is, however, appropriate to try and draw from the experiences of some countries such lessons as seem of enduring worth to others.

Two main variants of a prices and incomes policy may be distinguished. In the first the central organizations of employers and trade unions take it upon themselves to try and regulate wages, though not necessarily prices, without any formal participation by the Government in the regulation. In the second the Government plays a more active part, either with or without the help of one or more independent public agencies.

The prototype of an incomes policy conducted solely by the central organizations of employers and trade unions is to be found in Sweden. In the early fifties after a wage 'freeze' of two years, the Swedish Employers' Confederation and the Confederation of Swedish Trade Unions developed the practice of negotiating annually future wage increases for Swedish manual workers. The system has two important features: first, it attempts to arrange simultaneously settlements for the greater part of the Swedish

economy; second, it deliberately sets out to narrow the spread of pay differences, its methods of doing so becoming more and more refined with time, the range of differences among unions first being narrowed, thereafter among groups within unions, and finally even among individuals within a group. The second or 'solidarity' aspect of the system is dependent on the first or 'centralized' aspect. It requires central organizations of employers and unions possessing considerable power or influence over their constituent members, unlike the loose confederations of employers and unions in the United Kingdom and the United States. A decentralized system for determining pay increases, in which each union is free on its own to negotiate with a particular industry or particular firm, 'may preserve the problem of low wages and at the same time contribute to the rise in high-wage firms of what Engels and Lenin called a worker aristocracy'.*
The system tries to deal, therefore, with the problem of wage leadership through centralization. Judged by its own standard it is not, however, entirely successful; it does not extend to white collar workers; and the weakness of the centre was demonstrated in 1969 when some rank and file miners went on strike against their own union's wage negotiation. Nor does the system try and deal with the Government's view of what the country can 'afford' to pay by way of wage increases; many indeed are the tales of the Swedish Minister of Finance emerging from talks with the central organizations of employers and trade unions and wringing his hands in despair at their refusal to accept his analysis. This, no doubt, is a product of the voluntary nature of the system. Finally the system does not touch prices. It therefore seeks to face some of the causes of inflation, but not all.

As opposed to Sweden with its voluntary policy confined to incomes, the Western country which has been foremost in post-war history in active Government intervention in a policy is Holland. For the first post-war decade Dutch policy met with a considerable degree of success. Difficulties began to appear from the late fifties onwards. Those difficulties carried lessons, both as to the content of policy and as to the institutions for running a

* Rudolf Meidner and Berndt Öhman, *Fifteen Years of Wage Policy*, Swedish Trade Union Confederation, 1972, p. 41.

policy, for the British experiment of 1965–70 and its sequel. I cannot do better than quote from the Dutch economist, Jan Pen: 'A new cabinet with a slant to the right had appeared (in 1959). Freedom became a new goal ... overall economic policy and planning were to be pushed more into the background. "Greater responsibility for the separate sectors of industry" was the slogan.'* Pay in a sector was to reflect the productivity of that sector – true, with the qualification that fast-advancing sectors should to some extent also lower their prices. In the upshot, however, the spectacle of different rates of increase in productivity, and therefore in pay, placed too great a strain on people's notion of what was equitable. This was the very opposite of the 'solidarity' policy of Sweden and overlooked entirely the wage leadership problem described in Chapter Two.

The lessons as to the appropriate form of institutional arrangements is to be found in the shift, indeed a fragmentation, of authority which took place at the beginning of 1963. The agency regulating wages had been the Board of Government Mediators, an independent body which before the Second World War had indeed been concerned with just mediation or arbitration. On the morrow of the war there had also been established the Foundation of Labour, a body containing representatives of employers' associations and trade unions, and having as its aim the promotion of 'better understanding between the two sides of industry'. In 1963 the task of regulating wages was transferred from the Board of Mediators to the Foundation. To quote again from Professor Pen: 'The Board deliberately functioned as a scapegoat and it was well suited for this purpose. The Foundation of Labour is in a different situation. Now the employers and workers must themselves take this final decision. If tensions arise, they cannot be shifted to somebody else. The parties have the choice between conflict and wage inflation. But this choice is not a real one, because conflict within the Foundation always leads to pay rises in the long run. And, what is also important, they make people wish for a change in the system.'†

* Jan Pen, 'The Strange Adventures of Dutch Wage Policy', *British Journal of Industrial Relations*, November 1963.
† Jan Pen, loc. cit.

In due time a change in the system took place. In 1968 there was formed a new Wage Advisory Committee, chaired by the vice-chairman of the Board of Mediators. The Minister of Social Affairs could seek the opinion of the Committee about wage agreements if advised by the Board that they threatened economic stability, and he retained an ultimate sanction of invalidating the agreement. This was something akin to the British system of 1965–70, though the Wage Advisory Committee proved subsequently to be more obeisant to Ministers than was the British Prices and Incomes Board.

As far as institutions for a purely incomes policy were concerned, Holland thus covered the entire gamut – from reliance on an independent body, the Board of Mediators, she moved to dependence on employers and unions themselves, the Foundation of Labour, and then moved half-way back again to an advisory committee to a Minister.

One of the countries to attempt to cope with inflation by relying mainly on a policy for prices has been Canada; not that this was the original intention. In the spring of 1969 the Canadian Government set up a Prices and Incomes Commission, which came under the sponsorship of the Department of Consumer and Corporate Affairs, at that time the only Government department thus named in any country that I knew of. The Commission, which was largely modelled on its counterpart in the United Kingdom, sought to secure the voluntary agreement of trade unions and managements to a prices and incomes policy. After an exploratory period the trade unions withdrew their co-operation, while management continued for the time being to co-operate.

The agreement of managements was obtained at a National Conference on Price Stability in February 1970. For most of that year price increases were to be kept lower than cost increases; profits, that is, were to be squeezed. The Prices and Incomes Commission made investigations and issued reports on particular cases, usually on its own initiative without any reference from the Canadian Government. In the autumn of 1970 attempts were made to continue the experiment for the first six months of 1971. They failed, partly because the trade unions still refused to commit themselves, partly because managements wished to restore the profit margins that had been squeezed in 1970. The voluntary price restraint experiment launched in the United Kingdom in mid-1971 by the Confederation of British Industry had thus all been gone through before. The Canadian Commission had two roles: investigatory research and the giving of policy advice on the current situation. By the end of 1970 the Commission's latter role was substantially complete, while the research work and the framing of longer-range policy recommendations continued until August 1972. As part of this work the Commission prepared, at the request of the Government, a stand-by programme for immediate use in case of need. Just as the effort undertaken in the United Kingdom between 1965 and 1970 had in part inspired the Canadian effort, so the Canadian policies in turn played a role in shaping the programme introduced in the United States in August 1971.

France, like Canada, set up a weaker version of the British Prices and Incomes Board called the Centre d'Etudes pour les Coûts et les Revenus. Established in 1966, it simply provided a periodic statistical commentary on trends in costs and incomes, rather like the 1957 British Council on Prices, Productivity and Incomes. Any control on incomes was operated, not directly through a control of prices, but indirectly through a control on prices, more stringent than in Canada. Price control had been exercised in France throughout the post-war period, though undergoing different forms as circumstances changed. I first encountered it in 1967, when the United Kingdom was seeking how best to emerge from a situation of 'freeze'. France, it seemed to me, had then found a neat exit from a similar state of affairs.

Rather than restore full freedom to prices she had hit upon a system of contracts between the Government and sectors of industry. A sector was allowed to increase its prices by a given percentage provided it complied with certain demands made by the Government – for example, locating new capacity in one region rather than in another. After the student-cum-pay explosion of 1968, an explosion which in its turn may be partly attributed to too long a restriction of the economy and the accompanying unemployment, the system became less formal.

General pressure by the Government on the pricing policies of firms and sectors came to be substituted for the system of contracts, it being hoped that this pressure would bring about more effective pressure on incomes. The problem of income determination itself was left to research and study. There is no firm evidence that either the pressure on prices or the research reports had any great effect on the movement of incomes or of labour costs per unit of output.

The country which most closely studied the British experiment of 1965–70 and came to follow it, just as she had also preceded it, was the United States. She had had detailed control of prices and wages during the Korean war in the early fifties. In addition she had gone further than other countries in trying to ensure the maintenance, or the restoration, of the more fully competitive markets associated with the nineteenth century. Having had since the mid-1930's legislation designed to tilt the wage bargaining balance towards labour, she had on the morrow of the Second World War passed legislation to redress the balance somewhat towards management – the Taft-Hartley Act of 1947. She had also been more vigorous than other Western countries in the attempt to curb monopolies and restrictive practices by businesses. In particular America has been meticulous in following a view of Adam Smith's: 'People of the same trade seldom meet together, even for merriment and diversion, but the conversation ends in a conspiracy against the public, or in some contrivance to raise prices. It is impossible indeed to prevent such meetings, by any law which either could be executed, or would be consistent with liberty and justice.' British post-war legislation on both restrictive practices and monopolies has been more pragmatic. Whereas in the United States restrictive arrangements are unlawful *per se*, in the United Kingdom there is a rebuttable presumption that they are against the public interest. In the United States it is illegal to monopolize; in Britain a positive finding is required that size is inimical to the public interest.

Despite the pre-existence of legislation governing both industrial relations and industrial size the Kennedy Administration, which took office in 1961, still considered that it required something additional if it were to expand the economy and so reduce unemployment, then 7 per cent, without incurring inflation. Accordingly, the Annual Report for 1962 of the President's Council of Economic Advisers set out criteria to be observed by both trade unions and managements if a reduction in unemployment was not to be accompanied by an unacceptable rise in prices. These were later to be the criteria adopted in the United Kingdom in 1964–5. Actual or potential breach of the criteria was to be visited with the disapproval of the President and such counteraction as he could command – for example, the sale of strategic stocks held by the Administration. It was undoubtedly too much to ask of a President to intervene whenever the criteria were threatened with contravention; perhaps it was also too much to ask of a Council of Economic Advisers concerned in the main with problems of large economic magnitudes to intrude itself into the specific issues of this or that wage or price increase. Even so expansion and the reduction of unemployment were accompanied by reasonable price stability – whether because of the policy or not – until around 1965, when the demands of the war in Vietnam caused prices to accelerate sharply upwards.

This was the situation inherited by the Republican Administration presided over by Mr Nixon in November 1968. Mr Nixon, probably a pragmatic conservative by nature but affected by the intellectual climate of a country attached to the concept of a free market, set about the problem by traditionally orthodox means: a combination of tighter fiscal or tax and monetary policies. Not for him futile requests to recalcitrant trade unions leaders or chairmen, who, in pursuing the private interests of their constituents, might, according to nineteenth-century theory, be promoting also the public interest. His command over tax policy was far from complete: it was divided, according to the American Constitution, with Congress, which was converted only tardily to the Keynesian view that a Government's budget should be framed, not with a housekeeper's eye to an excess of revenue over expenditure, but with the wider objective of maintaining demand in the economy reasonably near the potential to produce. Nor was his command over monetary policy unambiguous, since the Federal Reserve Board, though appointed by the President, 'feels its primary responsibility is to Congress'; even so, President Nixon, like his predecessors throughout the post-war period in the United States, made greater use of monetary than of fiscal policy.

By 1970, however, monetary policy had reached its limit. If pushed too far, it can provoke a crisis of confidence. And it had brought about the bankruptcy of the Pennsylvania Central Railway. Mr Nixon then stepped back from the brink. Monetary policy was relaxed and Penn Central, the 'lame duck', was helped, just at the moment in time when the Conservative Government in the United Kingdom was on the point of promulgating the doctrine that 'lame ducks' should be left to their fate.

Meanwhile the net effect of the traditionally orthodox policies had been to increase unemployment to 6 per cent but without significantly abating inflation. And unemployment hit, possibly to a greater extent than in Great Britain, specific groups – the blacks, school leavers, married women. In August 1971 Mr Nixon acted contrary to all expectation. He did not, as did the Labour Government in the United Kingdom in 1964–5, introduce first a voluntary policy, to be followed later by one of compulsion. From the start he compelled. He ordained a 'freeze' of all prices and incomes, including dividends, for ninety days. During this time some 85,000 spot checks were undertaken by the Inland Revenue staff to ensure compliance. The 'freeze' was to be followed by a period of tight control, amounting to what would be termed in Britain a 'statutory policy', to last for an unspecified length of time.

How does one reconcile this *volte face* with the previous adherence to traditional policies? Intellectually this is not difficult. Mr Nixon could claim that he had inherited an inflation generated by a monetary demand in excess of the capacity to produce; all the figures suggested that he had eliminated this excess. However the expectation of continued inflation lived on. Hence the combination of high unemployment with rising prices. The 'freeze' and the statutory policy were needed to choke off the expectations. When once the expectations had been checked, the controls could be lifted and life could return to normal.

The theory may not be all that implausible. It may be that inflation disturbs the traditional relationships between different incomes, the relationships that are therefore accepted as fair; once started, the disturbance causes inflation to go on. If the disturbances can be smoothed out by some means, however novel, it is possible that traditional policies for maintaining stable prices can come into their own again, provided, of course, that there is no fresh source of disturbance. This is not, however, the moment to restate a view of inflation. Suffice it to say that a Republican Administration holding a political philosophy and therefore presumably a theory of inflation not fundamentally different from that of a Conservative Government in Britain resorted to a statutory policy, while its British counterpart continued stoutly to deny the need for one.

The methods by which the policy in the United States was carried out also differ significantly from those characterizing British policy. In Britain between 1965 and 1970 individual cases had been singled out by the Government and sent to the Prices and Incomes Board, thus making the selection of references appear arbitrary. By contrast no room for arbitrariness was left by the United States Administration in its statutory prices and incomes policy of 1971, the policy being reasonably comprehensive, with a clear demarcation of functions between the Administration, on the one hand, and the adjudicating bodies, on the other.

The Administration was represented by the Cost of Living Council, 'consisting of high Government officials and representing the President's direct interest'. It was assigned the 'responsibility of establishing broad goals, determining the coverage of the control program, overseeing enforcement, and coordinating the anti-inflationary effort in line with the overall goals'.* The goal it set was a reduction in the rate of inflation to 2–3 per cent by the end of 1972, a reduction to 'about half the pre-freeze rate'. The development of 'guidelines and standards' to attain this goal was to be in the hands of two bodies: the Price Commission, composed of seven 'public members', and a Pay Board of fifteen members, 'divided equally among business, labour, and public representatives'. (All but one of the trade union

* *Economic Report of the President*, Washington, 1972, p. 85.

representatives later left.) There were two bodies, possibly because there had been two concerned with prices and incomes in the Korean War, possibly because managements did not want to see participation by trade unions in the determination of prices. A 'rent advisory board' was created to help the Price Commission, while the pre-existing tripartite Construction Industry Stabilization Committee 'was placed under the authority of the Pay Board'.* The National Commission on Productivity was expanded and given the 'advisory role of ensuring that the entire stabilization program encouraged productivity growth'.

The Cost of Living Council decided that smaller economic units should not be required to give advance notice or to report price and wage increases which were consistent with the basic guidelines established by the Price Commission and Pay Board. The largest firms and employee groups were required to obtain advance approval for any change from the Commission and the Board while an intermediate group was required to report after wages or prices had been increased. Thus did the Cost of Living Council determine coverage and method of reporting, but without picking and choosing among those required to report.

The Price Commission, having been given a target of bringing down the rate of inflation to 2–3 per cent by the end of 1972, set a rule for average price increases across the economy of 'no more than $2\frac{1}{2}$ per cent per year'. Prices could be increased to reflect certain cost increases after taking into account improvements in productivity, but not to the point where they raised a firm's overall profit margin before tax above that earned in the best two of the three previous financial years. The profit margin is the ratio of profits to sales, and not the ratio of profits to funds invested as we defined the rate of profit in Chapter One. The same rule for profit margins also applied to wholesalers and retailers. And the customary percentage mark-up on products bought from manufacturers was to remain unchanged. The concentration on a firm's overall profit margin was justified on three grounds: first, it was still possible for a firm to increase its gross profits as production and sales increased and so obtain funds for investment;

* ibid.

second, competition was facilitated, for if an efficient firm were denied a price increase because that would raise its profit margin above the permitted level, other less efficient firms would have to keep their prices down; third, the problem normally associated with price control – namely, that while the price ceiling is respected, the quality of the product is allowed to depreciate – was circumvented.

The Pay Board for its part set a general standard for annual pay increases of 5½ per cent, the figure to be subject to periodic review. Three main exceptions were allowed: first, where there had been a close or 'tandem' relationship in pay with that of other groups; second, where it was thought necessary to attract and retain essential labour; third, where pay increases had averaged less than a certain figure – namely, 7 per cent – over the preceding three years. In no case was the exceptional pay increase to exceed 7 per cent. It will be seen that the first and third exceptions were designed to meet the same point as the exception to the British 'norm' between 1965 and 1970 – where pay had fallen behind that for similar work; but the American exceptions were more tightly defined. It is to be noted that there was no exception on grounds of extra effort or a direct contribution to improved productivity, as there had been in the United Kingdom. It was made clear by the Price Commission that it would not recognize wage increases which exceeded the Pay Board's standards and that it would 'look very carefully at any labor cost increase, even if allowed by the Pay Board'.

Breaches of the findings of both the Pay Board and the Price Commission were punishable with fines. Anyone, whether a person, business or trade union wilfully violating a regulation was subject to a maximum fine of $5,000 for each offence. It seems that each unit of a product sold at above the regulated price constituted an offence, so that a higher fine than $5,000 could be imposed. For the most part there was voluntary compliance, and little evidence of evasion. The Administration took steps to enforce penalties in a number of cases, but in the first year of the policy's operation at any rate the question of whether to do so against an important trade union did not arise.

The American arrangements for regulating prices and incomes

had one apparent disadvantage compared with the earlier British arrangements on which they were in part modelled. The separation of the two bodies – one to deal with pay, and one to deal with prices – gave rise initially to different approaches and therefore to friction between the two bodies. The Price Commission might consider that the Pay Board was too lenient in its handling of prices; contrariwise the Pay Board might regard the Price Commission as lax in the treatment of prices and thus aggravating the problem of pay. It is conceivable that with time the temptation for the one to blame its difficulties on the other diminished. Further, while room was allowed for trade union members on the Pay Board, there was none on the Prices Commission; the trade unions could legitimately argue that in this sense the arrangements were biased against them. This argument was substantially weakened in the spring of 1972 when most of the trade union members on the Pay Board walked out. Both bodies thus came to consist primarily of 'public' members.

The great merit, on the other hand, of the American system over the British lay in the fact that the Pay Board and the Price Commission were, within the coverage determined by the Cost of Living Council, comprehensive in scope. This meant that firms responsible for some 45 per cent of all sales in the United States had to seek the approval of the Price Commission before introducing price increases; while firms accounting for a further 5 per cent of all sales had to notify the Commission when putting price increases into effect. Similarly wage increases affecting some 10 per cent of all employees in the United States had to be approved by the Pay Board before they could take place; while those affecting a further 7 per cent of all employees had to be notified to the Board. Both within and outside this coverage pay and price increases were subject to spot checks by the officials of the Internal Revenue Service. This system differed radically from the British system of 1965–70, which required that all notification of pay and price increases should be to Government Departments, with the Government approving a large number, while withholding approval in other cases pending the outcome of a reference to the British Prices and Incomes Board.

Perhaps the essential difference between the two systems lay in the length of time which they had in mind for realizing their objectives; and this difference was in turn traceable to a different starting-point. The American system started with a 'freeze' backed by sanctions; it set out to maintain the success that can be obtained through a 'freeze', to the point where any exceptions from a pay norm had to be kept within numerically defined limits, any breach being again punishable by sanctions; it was, therefore, short-term in its outlook. The British system, by contrast, started by being 'voluntary' – there were no sanctions; as a result its objectives from the beginning became longer-term. For example, it saw pay escalating because of ancient piecework systems of payment which had lost their rationale; it sought, therefore, to lay down guidelines for the more effective operation of piecework systems. When a' freeze' was introduced, followed by a phase of control designed to secure the short-term gains of the 'freeze', the British system could not entirely lose its birth-mark. The difference is epitomized in the reports, on the one hand, of the American Pay Board and Price Commission, and those, on the other hand, of the British Prices and Incomes Board. The first were short numerical answers to applications for pay and price increases; the second were often longer, intent on securing a fundamental reform.

There is clearly room for both the short- and longer-term objectives. Without some apparent short-term success, though success in this context is not easy to define, any system for regulating prices and incomes will find it difficult to survive. Equally, without longer-term reform, a short-term success may prove fragile. For example, the acceptance of certain differences in pay as related to differences in the contents of jobs is an essential requisite of a long-term sense of fairness; but to move to a job-evaluation scheme would be difficult, if not impossible, under the American system. Ideally, therefore, a system ought to aim at attaining both the short- and longer-term ends. The problem is whether such a system is possible, whether worth-while longer-term ends can be purchased without a price which may be too high in the short term. It is difficult to give a categorical answer to this question, for few regulatory systems have attempted simultaneously to realize the short- and long-term objectives. All one can say is that the two can pull in different directions.

It was in fitting the system to the economic circumstances that the American government proved more skilful than the British. The United States effectively devalued the currency and simultaneously 'froze' prices and incomes; from the 'freeze' she moved, at first stumblingly then more assuredly, into a phase of statutory control; a year after the effective devaluation her record in price stability was much better than that of other countries. And a route to longer-term reform was opening before her. By contrast Britain in 1965 introduced a voluntary policy while demand was rising fast; she 'froze' and then controlled in an attempt to stave off devaluation; before devaluation came she relaxed and after devaluation she progressively abandoned the policy. In the ensuing rush such long-term reforms as the policy had started lay trampled. When a prices and incomes policy was re-introduced in the United Kingdom in 1972 the lessons of history had still not been entirely learned. Demand was again rising as in 1965; the pound sterling was effectively devalued in June 1972 when it was allowed to 'float' freely; talks were then started for a voluntary policy; they failed and a statutory freeze was introduced in November 1972. History suggests that the fact of devaluation and the protracted talks for a voluntary policy must have caused the inflation to accelerate.

No country so far mentioned, neither Sweden, nor Holland, France, Canada or the United States, has yet tried to integrate the older method of regulating disputes over the division of the national product – namely, conciliation or mediation between disputants in a pay claim – with the newer method – namely, prices and incomes policies. Through prescience or good fortune only one country has tried to do this – Australia. As long ago as 1904 she had hived off from the Government the function of finding the middle ground or conciliating between employers and unions. In that year there was established the Conciliation and Arbitration Commission. A management or a union in dispute could turn to the Commission and ask it to conciliate. If its answer by way of conciliation was not accepted, the Commission could compulsorily arbitrate – that is, it could indicate the settlement which it thought desirable. Only an arbitration award was legally binding on employers, but an appeal against the arbitration award could be made on limited grounds to a higher court. If the latter, however, upheld the award, any party still contesting it would be in contempt of court. If that party were a trade union, it would be liable to a fine if the Commission so directed.

Further, from the early days the Conciliation and Arbitration Commission had been given some guidance about the minimum size of an award. It had to give what was known as a 'living wage', conceived as a wage floor fixed by reference to family needs. Over time this came to mean a wage automatically rising as the cost of living rose – an automatic link that meant that an increase in the cost of living fed itself into a wage increase, which fed back again to the cost of living, and thus implied a tendency for inflation to go on. In the fifties the link had therefore to be abandoned. Despite these difficulties the Commission represented a vehicle both for conciliating and for determining the appropriate size of a pay award other than in terms of straight conciliation. Unlike other countries Australia had already to hand an instrument for applying an incomes policy. When, after 1945, the Australian Federal Government, like other governments, became interested in ensuring that pay settlements did not exceed a certain level, it was inevitable that it should attempt to get the Commission to observe a maximum rather than an outmoded minimum. This attempt reached its climax in a statement on 7 December, 1971, by the Australian Minister for Labour and National Service announcing an intention to amend the Conciliation and Arbitration Act: 'The Government will amend the Act to provide that . . . the Commission will be required to have regard to the likely national economic consequences of any award or order that it might make in settlement of a dispute.' As part of the amendment the 'conciliation' members of the Commission were separated from the 'arbitration' members, on the ground that, during conciliation, they would have learnt the innermost thoughts of the disputants; if conciliation fails, and the dispute therefore goes to arbitration, the arbitrators have now to approach the matter afresh.

This history contrasts sharply with that of the United Kingdom, where up to the end of 1972 the two policies of conciliation, on the one hand, and the regulation of incomes, on the other, remained distinct. The day was bound, however, to arrive when it was no longer possible to conceal the clash between the older function of government of refereeing a contest over pay and the newer interest of government in the outcome of the contest. Perception dawned in the early months of 1972, when trade unions and managements mooted the idea of a conciliation service *independent* of Government, an idea which they later put into effect. It was an unrealistic idea, ignoring both the interest of governments all over the world in the size of pay increases and the Australian effort to feed an incomes policy into an instrument originally set up for purposes of conciliation. The British Government, for its part, stayed passive, firmly caught in the dilemma of how to reconcile new functions with old.

What this account of policies in different countries shows is that there is no such thing as a single prices and incomes policy inviting universal condemnation. Diverse countries have diverse policies, all with their virtues and their defects. Sweden has a policy aiming at narrowing differences in income, but not necessarily taking account of the national capacity to pay. Holland has a policy which has undergone several phases, and any judgement has to be related to the particular phase. France has had, but no longer has, a tight policy on prices, and only the most general policy on incomes. Canada has had a voluntary policy on prices and none on incomes, and yet has prepared a 'stand-by' compulsory policy for both in case of need. The United States introduced, after a 'freeze', a compulsory policy on both prices and incomes, a policy which has fitted in with other policies and has been attended with short-term success, but which may possibly prove inimical to the longer-term reform of methods of determining pay.

Between 1965 and 1970 the United Kingdom did much pioneering, and other countries carefully noted her efforts. But in 1970 she swept everything away. She was harking back to a past which had irretrievably gone, while the rest of the world was evolving away from it. She has now to put the pieces together again, drawing the lessons which seem appropriate both from her own experience and the experience of other countries. They are surely these: the policy has to cover both prices and incomes; it has to take account of both economic and social forces; it has to pull with, and not against, other policies; it has to be integrated with a policy for industrial relations, not segregated from it; and it has to debate, more fully than has hitherto been the case in the United Kingdom, the issue of compulsion versus voluntarism.

Chapter Ten

The Adjudicator

During the earlier phase of history when the State saw its interest in the conflict between labour and capital as the keeping of the peace, the Government simply acted as the referee. It appointed *ad hoc* conciliators or arbitrators or placed at the disposal of the disputants its own conciliation service. In the later phase in which we are now living, when states have come to see that the conflict between capital and labour, even when peacefully resolved, can have adverse implications for the community and have therefore begun to develop prices and incomes policies, who shall be the referee or the adjudicator? Who, in other words, shall judge whether in fact prices and incomes are being determined in accordance with the criteria? Shall it be the central organizations of the employers and trade unions, seeking to influence and possibly correct the behaviour of their members, as is the case up to a point in Sweden? Shall it be some representative body of both, such as the Foundation of Labour in Holland? Shall it again be the Government who acts as referee or adjudicator on prices and incomes just as it has hitherto done in industrial relations? Or shall it be an 'independent' body such as the Prices and Incomes Commission of Canada, or the Pay Board and Prices Commission of the United States, or even the Conciliation and Arbitration Commission of Australia, combining conciliation with a 'regard to the likely economic consequences of any award'? And if it is an 'independent' body, whether its purview relates only to prices and incomes or encompasses both prices and incomes and industrial relations, what are the political and constitutional implications of such a body?

Let us consider, first, adjudication by the central organizations of the employers and trade unions, or by some joint body representative of both. Bodies such as the Trades Union Congress or the Confederation of British Industry could potentially order their members to conform to certain rules. Whether they could do this effectively or not would depend very much on tradition; and traditionally the TUC and the CBI in the United Kingdom have regarded themselves only as loose confederations claiming no power of command. Even so, in the period 1965–70 the TUC did for some time have a 'vetting' committee which scrutinized the pay claims of individual unions. I can express no opinion on the effectiveness of the committee's work, for nothing was known of it publicly. The CBI, on the other hand, did not seek to influence the pricing decisions of its member firms, beyond being a signatory on their behalf to the compact to abide by the criteria. By the early 1970s the boot was on the other foot. The TUC had dismantled its 'vetting' committee, while the CBI, first in 1971 and again in 1972, persuaded most of its 200 largest members to limit their price increases. Potentially, then, the central organizations of managements and unions can do something. The rub is that, however honestly they acted, they would never be regarded by the outside world as acting impartially. If the regulation of prices were left to the central organization of managements, would the community of consumers be satisfied? If the regulation of wages were left entirely to the central organization of trade unions, would society be ready to place trust in it? A CBI and a TUC can play a useful supporting role; but by definition they cannot be sole adjucators, for they would be adjudicating on their own behalf. And if it were a question of judging between individual constituent members, who would believe that decisions were not governed by the play of power within the organizations and that the big battalions were not calling the tune?

What then of a joint body representative of both, like the Dutch Foundation of Labour? This merely takes us back to our old problem – the actions of employers and unions in unison can be against the interests of the community. A pertinent comment on this was quoted from Professor Pen on page 144. We can only conclude that sole adjudication by central organizations of managements and workers or a joint body representative of both would be suspect as not holding the scales evenly and is not therefore a satisfactory answer.

Let us ask ourselves next whether the Government could be a suitable adjudicator. The Government determines global economic policy, but, being subject to election, policy is influenced by its interpretation of the public wish, whether that interpretation be right or wrong. The Government is primarily responsible for the level of Government spending. It also exercises a considerable influence over the supply of credit, though there are forms of credit that can elude Governmental control. But we have seen that Governments have a tendency to inflate the level of their spending and the supply of credit with the approach of elections. In between elections, however, there are matters on which Governments turn to an external judge. For example, in the United States the President, when faced with a prospective strike that carries with it the threat of a national 'emergency', sets up a fact-finding board before using his power to order the parties to 'cool off'. In the United Kingdom, the Government, having passed legislation to deal with monopolies, has set up a permanent Monopolies Commission to judge individual cases which the Government may refer to it. And from time to time, on such explosive issues as the siting of a third London airport, the Government has established an *ad hoc* commission of enquiry to make a recommendation, though the Government has retained a power to over ride the recommendation. In short, Governments often resort to the device of some kind of external authority to help ensure that their actions appear 'fair'.

This appearance of 'fairness' is all the more important in the field of prices and incomes. The Government itself determines not only the incomes of its own employees, but also certain important prices in the public sector. The Government is thus identified in the public mind with the incomes paid to and the prices charged by a large sector of the economy. It would scarcely seem 'fair' for the Government to pose as the judge of whether or not it was adhering to the criteria. More significant still, in countries such as the United Kingdom and the United States the Government is formed from one of two parties; of the two, one is loosely identified with labour, the other with capital; even on the assumption of some kind of compact with managements and trade unions on how any increase in the national income should be divided, a Government of any colour would run the risk of not appearing neutral. This risk would be increased by the fact that it was operating in a two-party system, with the party in Opposition ready and more than willing to pounce on any apparent departure from neutrality. This point has been well put by the Canadian Task Force on Industrial Relations in 1968 when it proposed that an independent commission, and not the Government, should handle disputes where the public interest was threatened. 'There remain the dangers of political pressures or accusations of partiality that jeopardise the settlement of disputes when they arise.' To leave the decision to the Canadian Department of Labour, it was said, would be to endanger its role as independent conciliator and to put the Department on one side of the conflict.* This argument for an independent commission was advanced in the context of industrial relations. But it is equally valid in the context of prices and incomes.

Throughout the years 1965–70 the Government in the United Kingdom retained the exclusive right to determine the cases to be judged by the Prices and Incomes Board. The Board could suggest cases, privately and indeed sometimes (in the course of its General or Annual Reports) openly; but the Government ultimately selected. And this right of selection implied a prior judgement by the Government. How then was this judgement exercised?

The question is not easy to answer. The Government never gave publicly its reasons for referring or not referring. Frequently, around the circuit of Whitehall information, there would come signals to the effect that the Government (meaning civil service officials) was contemplating this or that reference. Occasionally, though generally after some time, the contemplation would indeed emanate in a reference. Sometimes it would just peter out or conceivably meet with a negative decision by the Cabinet or the relevant Cabinet sub-committee; since one was not privy to

* Quoted from Otto Kahn-Freund and Bob Hepple, *Laws against Strikes*, Fabian Society, 1972, p. 25.

Ministerial discussions one was never quite sure which. Nor, for the same reason, did one know the thinking lying behind a negative Ministerial decision. A Minister, not necessarily the Minister in charge of the prices and incomes policy, but a Minister preoccupied with a problem, might, in private conversation with me, ventilate the possibility of this reference or that, the idea probably being his own rather than that of officials; I would respond as I thought fit. And sometimes a reference would come to the Board out of the blue, without previous preparation by officials or intimation by Ministers; this was generally a sign of Prime Ministerial intervention. In this state of ignorance one can only speculate about what moved Government in its work of prior judgement; but it was an unfortunate situation.

While the Board was born of a compact between the Government, the Confederation of British Industry and the Trades Union Congress, the main parent was the Government. The Government was therefore anxious that the compact should work and so the earlier cases sent to the Board were those thought to be relatively easy. This inevitably meant that more 'difficult' cases, in the sense of the highest pay and prices increases, continued to have an intractable influence after the Board had begun to function. As and when the more difficult cases began to arrive, the Board had already established something of a reputation for the quality of its reports. It appeared therefore to stand a chance of fulfilling the belief that a policy without sanctions might lead to more 'enlightened' behaviour; that is, behaviour in the longer-term, not just the shorter-term, interests of firms and trade unions. For this reason it was the view of both Government and Board officials that the number of references to the Board should be kept limited, so that the Board might concentrate on its reports and thus discharge its enlightening mission. And this view persisted even after the introduction of sanctions. Is a policy better conducted through fuller judgements on a limited number of cases or through more summary judgements on a far wider range of cases? In the United Kingdom the former was the case; in the United States we have seen that it was the latter, the Pay Board and the Prices Commission being comprehensive in their purview. My answer now would be that the American system is the better, provided that it can be coupled with, as I believe it can, fuller reports on subjects calculated to promote longer-term reform of the institutions determining pay and prices.

After the devaluation of the pound in November 1967, the prices and incomes policy, while remaining in being with the full rigour of sanctions, was in practice relaxed, the relaxation being particularly marked after the transfer of responsibility for the policy in the spring of 1968 from the Department of Economic Affairs to the new Department of Employment and Productivity. As far as references to the Board were concerned, the relaxation showed itself in two ways. Many pay increases notified to the Department of Employment as being above the standard but held to be justified on grounds of increased productivity were not referred to the Board; whether they were in fact justifiable I do not know, since the Board never examined them. And the references that were made became less specific and more general in character: they required not so much a judgement on a particular claim as an examination of the pay and conditions in an industry. References of this kind implied a belief that research, and the information and guidance to which it can give rise, can contribute to enlightened behaviour more effectively than judgement on a specific issue. A similar belief would seem to have inspired the creation of the Office of Manpower Economics after the return of the Conservatives to power in 1970.

Now research and the guidance stemming therefrom can indeed be useful, but rather in the longer than in the shorter term. The Board's Report on *Payment by Results* showed the laxity with which many systems of payment by results were conducted to be an important source of rising labour costs per unit of output. The Report accordingly set out guidelines to help bring about and maintain a tighter administration of such systems of payment. But tighter administration in the future might need to be bought at a higher cost now. Similarly the introduction of schemes of evaluating jobs and reviews of the entire structure of salaries can remove the sense of grievance which often gives rise to competitive wage claims. But they may need to be accompanied by a sharp initial increase in pay. Long-term reform does not therefore displace the need for a judgement now as to how much extra pay shall be granted in a particular case. And the immediate requirement may place a limit to the price which should now be paid for longer-term reform, just as in American policy a maximum was put to any exceptional pay increase. Thus both short-term issues and longer-term requirements have to come under the scrutiny of the same independent judge, for participation in the act of adjudication by the Government will make for the contradictions described in Chapter Seven.

How did it come about that the Government, having set up an independent, non-elected, body to examine individual pay and price decisions in the light of criteria agreed upon with managements and trade unions, chose, at different times and varying degree, not to seek its judgement? The Government, as the sole source of references, played the principal part in the act of judgement. Why? The superficial answer is that the Government might have hesitated to create too large an external organization; although subsequent American experience suggests that the organization need not have been all that large.

Perhaps the deeper answer is that the British are more suspicious than most other nations of anything which appears to derogate from the supremacy of a popularly elected Government. Certainly suspicion was expressed of the Board as a body of growing influence without electoral responsibility. This suspicion misconstrued the relationship between the Board and the Government. The Board's function was to adjudicate and recommend. It was for the Government to act or not to act on the recommendation; to disregard it, to persuade parties to accept it, or to enforce it. The Board was constrained to operate within certain rules and guidelines. The establishment of those rules and guidelines was the responsibility of the elected Government, preferably with the consent of all parties affected.

We have established that the adjudicator cannot be the central organization of employers, nor of the trade unions, nor can it be the Government; the adjudicator has to be independent. Participation by the Government in the act of adjudication through, for example, the choice of references makes for contradiction and confusion, and indeed renders the position of the adjudicator ultimately untenable. We have yet to address ourselves, however, to the question whether the adjudicator might not in some way be three-sided, say, a sub-committee of a body such as the National Economic Development Council, containing a member of the Government, a member of the CBI and a member of the TUC. The answer to this question is to be found in the history of the period 1965–70. Alongside the investigations undertaken by the Prices and Incomes Board certain pay claims were 'vetted' by the TUC and proposed pay and price increases were scrutinized by Government Departments. But the Board was more faithful to the criteria than either of the other two judges. The reason lay deeper than in the formal requirement placed upon it to pay regard to the criteria. The Board had been established to look at cases in the light of the compact reached at the end of 1964 between the Government, the Trades Union Congress and the Confederation of British Industries. The signatories themselves might have reasons, good or bad, at different moments of time, for breaking with the compact. The TUC wished to break with it in the face of the attempted legislation on strikes. The Government wished to break with it as the General Election of 1970 approached. The CBI wished to break with it when the outcome of the Election was known and wage costs were escalating. But the Board had no other *raison d'être* than to adjudicate in accordance with the compact. Its self-interest lay solely in continuing to guard the policy, even when others were departing from it.

Not that it could afford to be entirely rigorous in this attempt. There were reasons why it too had on occasion to disregard the criteria, masking its action as best it could. It had none of the tradition that had clustered round older bodies, such as Wages Councils; arbitration courts, some established by law; or special review committees or commissions concerned with the remuneration of a particular profession and jealously guarded by that profession unto itself. These bodies, acting generally in accordance with the philosophy reigning at their moment of birth, paid little regard to the criteria which the Board was required to observe. Their longer lineage kept them aloof. More important still, the Government, not as judge but as employer, frequently and increasingly with time, broke its own rules. When it laid down a maximum it treated it, in relation to its own employees, as a minimum; and from the autumn of 1969 onwards it was settling well above any White Paper figure. Amidst the surrounding inconsistency the Board, in its acts of judgement, had to temper its custody of the policy with realism. And this inevitably meant that its acts of adjudication were different from those of a legal judge.

Judgements in industrial relations, in disputes between employees and trade unions, seldom permit of exact answers. The issues cannot be answered by a straight 'Guilty' or 'Not guilty'. The same is true of answers on prices and incomes. This lack of legalism in the nature of the answers was reinforced by chance. I myself had no legal background; I did not know, and did not try to adopt, the formal ways of a court. And, as stated earlier, the disposition to endorse an exception from the standard figure on the ground of an exceptional contribution to improved productivity reflected the initial voluntary nature of the policy: the nervousness that a 'No' unbacked by law might be rebuffed; the pressure being therefore to seek a qualifying answer. These, however, were accidents. More importantly, the price–wage spiral itself forced the Board into giving larger answers than 'Yes' or 'No'. First there was the rolling nature of the inflationary problem, the fact that a pay claim arising on the morrow of the policy had its origin in a pay settlement reached or a price determined before the policy began, that a price increase put forward during the policy reflected costs incurred before the policy was known; secondly, there was the fact that the current judgements and actions of bodies other than the Board were paying scant heed to the policy. Hemmed in by both the past and the present, the Board certainly had to look at pay and prices in the light of the criteria, but also to reconcile its scrutiny, if this were indeed possible, with events that had gone before or that were going on now. In more concrete terms this reconciliation could be effected only if it could be shown that previous costs or costs currently arising could be absorbed and that pay, past and present, should be viewed more comprehensively.

It was this realization of the farther-reaching implications lying behind any one reference on pay or prices that led the Board, from the very beginning, to set itself the task of being thoroughly 'expert' – to use consultants; to enlist academics, who helped with the adoption of survey techniques; and to recruit as far as it could from industry, though the main source of recruitment remained, to the end, the Civil Service. The Board, in effect, took up the role of a spur to the containment of rising wage costs and prices in the future. This led in September 1967 to the Board's being formally requested to undertake 'efficiency audits' of nationalized industries in conjunction with an examination of any proposals for major price increases by them. There would have been brought down from the past a legacy of costs, or there were, streaming in from the present, costs arising outside the Board's judgement; in the shorter term these costs were difficult to carry without an effect on prices; in the longer term, however, there could be an adaptation to them, without an erosion of profits or an increase in prices, provided certain courses of action were taken. To help it recommend the requisite methods the Board recruited a wider range of experts, chiefly from the private sector; and this influx was beginning to show fruit when it was announced in the autumn of 1970 that the Board was to be abolished.

The Board's particular interpretation of its adjudicating function and its chosen way of discharging it have a many-sided significance. They have a significance, first, for the techniques employed in the various enquiries required by Government, particularly in the field of pay and prices. Before the inception of the Board it was the practice in the United Kingdom and it has been the practice since the Board's demise, to head such enquiries with a Judge. It is demanded of a Judge in his walk of life that he be objective; not that he is the only one of whom in his avocation the rare trait of objectivity is expected. The Judge proceeds about his task by obtaining evidence from the 'parties' and submitting the latter to interrogation. The Board acted very differently. It sent into a firm, a nationalized corporation or a trade union, enquiry teams drawn from various disciplines; their questionnaires often being drawn up in agreement with the heads of the organization. More often than not the information brought back was unknown to the 'parties' and could not have been ascertained through formal evidence; for example, such information as the ranges of actual earnings or the use made of overtime. The Board drew its conclusions from relatively small statistical samples, unlike the large mass of statistical data compiled, often without reference to any particular problem, by most Government Departments. Nor was the enquiry confined to the parties; often it was extended to organizations which did not form part of the reference but which might, from a different experience, have a lesson for the problem in question. Enough was done to suggest that in matters of arbitration, or conciliation, or scrutiny of monopolies, the judicial approach is not the most suitable. This informal approach was not necessarily inconsistent with the principles of 'natural justice', which require that a party be informed of, and be given a chance to reply to, statements made about him.* Parties were in fact shown the 'factual' parts of reports relating to them as distinct from the recommendations.

Enough was done, second, to suggest that society has need of a permanent independent team constantly developing its methods of enquiry and its expertise, rather than a number of *ad hoc* and essentially amateur enquiry teams unable, because of their impermanence, to develop their methods. For example, one of the last investigations undertaken by the Board was into the profits of commercial television contractors. These last receive their franchise from an Independent Broadcasting Authority, and in exchange for the franchises, pay a levy which goes into the Government's general revenue. The Board's investigation was prompted by a squeeze on the contractor's profits and therefore by a plea that the levy should be reduced. There were three parties to the issue: the contractors who wanted the levy cut, if not waived; the Authority, influenced by the views of the contractors; and the Government, which wanted the levy retained. The Board, as the investigator, alone had no vested interest in the outcome, and it built on the methods developed in countless other enquiries to assess how far profits might be maintained. It could

* See Bob Hepple, *Race Relations and the Law*, Penguin, 1972.

similarly have gone on, and this is a hypothetical case, to consider whether costs justified any application by the British Broadcasting Corporation for an increase in the licence fee charged to viewers and listeners.

The Board's history had a significance, third, for the relationship between Government and industry, public or private. Government Departments have usually not been critical supervisors of the investment proposals of nationalized industries, largely because of the different experiences and therefore different languages of departmental officials and industrial executives.* The same comment is probably true of departmental reaction to proposals from industries nominally private but in receipt of public funds – for example, the aerospace industry. Like a department, the Board's staff were drawn in the main from governmental officials. For purposes of enquiry, however, even the governmental officials were chosen from departments accustomed to pursue lines of questioning; for example, Customs and Excise, and the Inland Revenue. While with the Board they were trained, or were encouraged to obtain qualifications, in such fields as industrial engineering, market research, and work study. The enquiry teams were led by carefully selected managers with experience in industry at a senior level, for these alone would command the respect and confidence of industrial management. And their work was integrated into reports and into Board policy by administrative officials. The Board thus, through a deliberate blend of a wide variety of competences, began to develop the nucleus of a more effective assessor of industry, public and private, than the usual Government Department.

Fourth, the width of the Board's enquiries was beginning to elicit the cooperation of trade unions. In so far as the reference allowed it to, the Board could enquire, not only into the utilization of labour, but also into efficiency in distribution, the purchasing and use of materials, or the level and the composition of overheads. These non-labour matters were often of great interest to

* See Aubrey Jones, Minutes of evidence taken before the Select Committee on Nationalized Industries, Subcommittee A, HC 371-II, July 1968 pp. 677–708.

trade unions, for they were relevant to the costs per unit of output, to the future of an industry or firm and therefore to the context within which wage negotiations took place.

Finally, the interpretation given by the Board to its function of adjudicator is pertinent to that never-ending debate on the economics of the market mechanism versus State control. The market-oriented economist would have it that resources are most effectively used when a number of freely competing firms respond to the price signals given in the market-place; the role of the State, he would say, is 'confined' to removing the obstacles to the freedom of response. The work of the Board showed that this is much too narrow a viewpoint. A State agency, by achieving a concentration of rare skills and by being careful not to become too 'theoretical', can help an industry towards greater efficiency. As an external body it can stimulate new ideas and act as an extra competitive force. There were few industries that did not appear to welcome this aspect of the Board's work, though they might have preferred it to be unrelated to a prices and incomes policy. For my part I do not believe that the Board could have played this role had it not been asked to answer the specific question whether this or that pay or price increase should or should not be allowed.

The Board's answers to the questions put to it were in part short-term: the relevant pay or price increase was or was not in accord with the criteria; in part long-term: the criteria could be complied with in some other way. Both parts of the answer were advisory to the Government, for it was the Government that had put the question. It was then for the Government to accept or reject the advice, and, if it accepted, to take the action on from there.

Let us consider the short-term answer first. In the voluntary phase the Government could do no other than try and persuade the parties to the Board's view that the settlement or the proposed increase in pay or prices did not conform with the criteria. I can recall no significant instance when it in fact failed to do so. Its success could, however, be ascribed to the relatively novel nature of the policy and the relatively short duration of the voluntary phase – roughly one year. One can only speculate as to whether the Government would have been equally successful had the voluntary phase lasted longer.

In the compulsory phase the Government could initially – 1966 to 1967 – fine if it found the criteria breached. Later it could seek to fine only if the Prices and Incomes Board, on a reference to it, judged the criteria to be broken. The fine was applicable either to individuals, employers or employees, in which case it was subject to a maximum, or to a body corporate, that is, a firm or trade union. Again I can recall no case in which a fine, either on the basis of a direct judgement by the Government or of a judgement by the Board, was in fact levied.

In practice, therefore, as far as short-term judgements were concerned, there was no great difference between the voluntary and compulsory phases, no open defiance in the first and no open penalty arising out of defiance in the second. This relative absence of difference does not, however, carry any significant lesson as to whether a policy with or without sanctions is the more effective. This basic question remains unanswered by the British experiment of 1965–70.

The conclusion to which British experience points is a more complicated one. As far as prices and incomes were concerned, Government in the United Kingdom was confused in its intentions. By tradition it was a conciliator between employers and trade unions; as a custodian of the country's gold and foreign exchange reserves it was prepared to buy off strikes at the expense of any incomes standard; as the instrument of a belief that a Government elected by universal franchise expresses the public interest it was jealously retentive of its powers; in any emergency it therefore set itself up as both prosecutor and judge if it deemed its standard infringed; yet in moments of something less than crisis the sanctions were applicable only on the expression of a judgement by an independent Board. Amidst all this confusion there was every likelihood that action taken in some cases would be contradicted by other cases. The sanctions were scarcely therefore applied.

As far as the longer-term recommendations of the Board were concerned – how best to meet the criteria over a longer term by, for example, a revision of the pay structure or the containment of costs through a reshaping of the distribution network – there was from the start a dispute as to who should assume the task of ensuring that they were observed. I wanted the task assumed by the Board, for otherwise I could never be sure of securing compliance. If, for instance, the Board recommended that a pay settlement for provincial printers could be justified if labour were re-deployed, I wanted a report after an interval of time to indicate what had been accomplished and an examination of the report by the Board. On the other hand, Mr George Brown, the Minister initially in charge of the Department of Economic Affairs, considered that the pursuit of the longer-term recommendations should be by him, on the valid ground that the Board should not delve too deeply into any one case but spread itself horizontally over many cases. This issue was the subject of the only major dispute I ever had with Mr George Brown.

The assumption by Government of the task of following up longer-term recommendations meant that, on the removal of responsibility for the policy from the Department of Economic Affairs, the function fell to the Productivity part of the new Department of Employment and Productivity. I cannot say that I was kept well informed of any action in this respect taken by the Department of Employment and Productivity; nor am I convinced that much action was taken at all. And towards the end of the Board's life the task neglected by Government was informally taken up by the Board itself.

In the main, however, the long-term effects which the Board wrought were the result, not solely of deliberate effort by Government or Board, but also of the fact that the recommendations were in keeping with the way in which events were moving. The Board's recommendations on clearing banks, published in 1967, were finally carried out in 1971. Those on solicitors' fees, first published in 1968, were acted on in 1972, after the Board had gone. And it is possible that the steady pressure of the Board's reports contributed to the 'shake-out' of labour that continued from 1966 to 1972, though it is to be regretted that there was no full-employment policy to take up the 'slack'.

At the outset I considered the Board's long-term recommendations to be all-important. Hence my opinion that the Board should play its part in ensuring that they were carried out. But I soon changed my view. The long-term recommendations were important, yes; but all-important, no. They could not be divorced from the short-term judgement on a particular case. The really important thing was to ensure that this judgement was made 'independently', away from party politics. And here we begin to touch the heart of a major political problem.

Chapter Eleven

The Politics of
Non-Partisanship

When I assumed the Chairmanship of the Prices and Incomes Board, I adopted, in a country with a two-party political system, a non-partisan stance. By most people non-partisanship is accepted for the monarchy, as standing beyond the political parties; for the armed forces and the civil service, as servants of the party temporarily ruling as the Government; and for the judiciary as an independent arm of Government. There are, in fact, a number of positions which need to be filled by non-partisans, by people who can operate under a Government of either party – for example, the Chairmanship of the Board of a nationalized undertaking, the Governorship of a central bank or of a public broadcasting authority, the Commissionership of a European Economic Community. The occupants of posts such as these need to be non-partisan for one or both of two reasons. Organizations such as a central bank have to continue in being whatever the party regime; it would be disruptive of the organization if the head were changed every time a party was changed. In addition some consistency of policy is often desirable; and in foreign affairs in particular a country has frequently to show a united front to the outside world.

The number of posts requiring non-partisan occupants seems likely to increase. For one thing, as certain activities of Government come to be accepted by both political parties, they may be hived off into independent organizations – for example, the running of a national medical service, the head of which has then to continue in office after the party that appointed him may have passed into opposition. For another, the world is contracting; bridges have to be thrown between countries; there has to be some coordination of policies on such subjects as pollution and currency exchange rates. Developments such as these require non-partisanship not only in the sense of continuity as national political parties alternate in office, but also in the sense of an ability to stand outside any one particular country. The European Economic Commission in Brussels is, for example, non-partisan in that it is required to present to sovereign States a wider and longer-term view than their own immediate interests might indicate.

In the contexts so far mentioned the desirability and feasibility of non-partisanship are seldom questioned. When, however, it comes to the distribution of income and wealth, a question which represents a great deal of the stuff of politics (though not necessarily the whole of it), the possibility of non-partisanship is less readily conceded. The need for it has none the less come to be accepted in some countries other than the United Kingdom. Industrial relations, for example, have partly to do with the distribution of income and wealth. And we saw in the last chapter how the Canadian Task Force on Industrial Relations had proposed that it should be an independent Public Interest Disputes Commission rather than either the Government or even the courts, * which should make recommendations in the case of disputes in which the 'public interest' was threatened. The Commission, in other words, was to be non-partisan.

A prices and incomes policy has similarly to do with the distribution of income and wealth. Strictly speaking it is confined to the manner in which the annual *increase* in the national income shall be apportioned, both between labour and capital, and between different groups of workers, different firms, and consumers. In dealing with the apportionment of the *increase*, however, it begins to touch on the general distribution of income and wealth. For example, a prices and incomes policy which gives a prior claim on the annual *increase* in the national income to the lower paid begins to divert a greater share of income to the poorer. Similarly, a prices and incomes policy such as that obtaining in Canada in 1970 which lays down that costs previously incurred

* Otto Kahn-Freund and Bob Hepple, *Laws Against Strikes*, Fabian Society, 1972, p. 25.

shall not be fully reflected in prices reduces the return on capital or the rate of profit.

The policy has to be concerned with the distribution of the *increase* in the national income because different parts of the economy grow at different speeds. Those parts growing fastest have it in their power to set the pace in increases in pay or profits; other more slowly growing parts then try to catch up in their pay or profits, with the result that prices rise and there is inflation. Since this is how the system works when left to itself, there has to be some form of intervention. The intervention suggested is guidance in the form of a set of rules or criteria, drawn up by the Government of the day in consultation with firms and trade unions, on how the *increase* in the national income shall be divided. The task of looking at particular cases in the light of the rules has to be entrusted to an independent body, independent, that is, of the Government, of particular firms and particular trade unions. The body is thus non-partisan in both the political and the industrial sense. Outside the policy the political parties can continue their debate, though the debate will be affected, and indeed restricted, by the policy itself. A radical party, for example, can still press for higher taxation on profits, a conservative party can still argue for greater differentiation of incomes at the top, though both will find that the existence of a policy puts limits to the extent to which they can push their case. In this sense partisanship can go on. A prices and incomes policy itself, however, if it embodies agreed rules on distribution, is non-partisan. But it has not so far been regarded as such.

In the United Kingdom the prices and incomes policy of 1965–70, despite its origins in efforts by both the main political parties, came to be identified with the Labour Party. It was cast out by the Conservative Party on its return to office. Two years later the Conservative Government itself was faced with the need to restore it. In the United States the Kennedy 'guide-post' policy was discarded by President Nixon, who none the less in his turn introduced a tougher policy. Clearly no policy will be effective and no organization as the vehicle for carrying out a policy can survive unless there is broad acceptance by both the main parties in a two-party system. Acceptance means not only continuance as parties alternate in office but also restraint in opposition as parties alternate in opposition. Let us then consider more closely the meaning of non-partisanship, how far the term can be applied to the divisive problem of prices and incomes, and how far a prices and incomes policy can be reconciled with different positions in the political spectrum.

Men live in society. The social unit may be small or large – a family, a nation, a community of nations, a world. But whatever the size of the unit the fact of living in a society imposes on an individual a condition: he can realize himself or promote his interests only if he also respects the interests of others and their entitlement to realize themselves. This mutual inter dependence of human beings holds them together in a compact. And the idea of a compact has been expressed by writers from all parts of the political spectrum. Thus, to quote from the Right: ' . . . society is neither more nor less than a compact . . . . They [the great statesmen of the past] knew that the foundation of civil polity is Convention, and that everything and every person that springs from that foundation must partake of that primary character.' * Similarly to quote from the contemporary Left: ' . . . we are members of one another. Our selves are not contained in our skins, but learnt from the people around us in reciprocal human action.' † And finally, from a philosopher whose political position is not so easily identifiable: 'however mistaken the notion of the social contract may be as history, and however far it may overreach itself as a general theory of social and political obligation, it does express, suitably interpreted, an essential part of the concept of justice.' ‡

The idea of society as held together by a compact or consensus is valid no matter what the particular economic institutions may be – whether workers are craftsmen each producing his own product, or operatives herded together in factories, drilling holes in

* Benjamin Disraeli, 'Vindication of the English Constitution', 1835, reprinted in *Whigs and Whiggism: Political Writings by Benjamin Disraeli*, edited by William Hutcheon, John Murray, 1913, pp. 123–4.

† Ken Coates and Tony Topham (eds.), *Workers' Control*, Panther Modern Society, 1970, p. 440.

‡ John Rawls, 'Justice as Fairness', *Philosophical Review*, Vol. LXVII, 1958, pp. 192–3.

sub-components of components to be assembled into finished products elsewhere; whether capital is owned publicly or privately; whether industry is controlled only by managers or whether control is shared between managements and workers or exercised solely by workers. The contractual view of society is too fundamental to be affected by changing economic forms. It is at the root of rules of behaviour which we all accept as applicable to ourselves – I accept that I may not assassinate my neighbour: 'morality must at least imply the acknowledgement of principles as impartially applying to one's own conduct as well as to another's, and moreover principles which may constitute a constraint, or limitation, upon the pursuit of one's own interest.' *
If I accept rules limiting my behaviour, I must also accept that the rules are observed. To ensure their observance I look to a jury which is not identified with any one person's interest, which recognizes that there is a restriction on the pursuit of everyone's interest, and which is, therefore, the repository of the consensus. In other words, the jury is non-partisan. And it is the recognition of a consensus which makes it possible for it to be non-partisan.

What is true of the basic rules of social behaviour is also true in a large measure of rules governing behaviour in prices and incomes. Rules on prices and incomes are required because, if those groups in the best position to extract high increases in pay and profits pursue their self-interest to the limit, both the resulting inflation and the attempt to conquer it will go far to nullify their efforts; besides hurting the weaker, therefore, they also do little to benefit themselves. The purpose of the rules is to remind them of the bounds beyond which, in their own interests as well as those of society, they should not go. The jury to which the observance of the rules is entrusted is non-partisan in that it stands outside any particular group and is there to apply the rules to all. If there is difficulty in accepting this idea it is because of the existence of two diametrically opposed political viewpoints: that which rejects the validity of any claim to profit and that which sees the mainspring of economic activity as the maximization of profit. Let us, therefore, look at the problem from different points in the political spectrum.

* John Rawls, 'Justice as Fairness', p. 172.

The 'revolutionary' Left sees that there is a difference between the total value created by labour and the wages received by labour. This difference, which we described in Chapter One as profits, is seen by the Left as 'exploitation'. 'Does it [labour] not deserve the whole product? . . . profits are not paid *for* anything, and serve no essential economic function.'* In so far as profits serve to allocate capital between this activity and that, it would be contended that this could be done by economic planning (which might be guided by a notional rate of return) rather than by any actual payment of profit. The aim of the Left, therefore, is to lift from labour the burden of paying profit. If the burden of profit could indeed by removed, then it is true that wages could increase faster than the increase in the gross domestic product without causing inflation.

The point of view just described contains, however, two basic weaknesses. First, profit never has been completely eliminated: 'When the workers voted for the Labour Government in 1945 they did so in the belief that the nationalization of the basic industries would take the burden of rent, interest and profit off the back of the industry, but in the nationalization of the coal industry, of the Bank of England, of the gas industry and the other industries we find that the principle adopted is that the ex-owners of the industries are guaranteed more or less the same amount of money in the form of compensation as they were getting before in the form of dividends.'† Not only this, but also the nationalized industries have to continue to finance at least a part of their investment from the surplus of output over wages. Nor, in the days of the multi-national corporation, is profit likely to be completely eliminated. We saw in Chapter Six how multi-national firms aim at a uniform world price, and are able to expand here or contract there, depending on the difference between the price and local costs – that is, the rate of profit in a particular country. Profit in any one country could not in these circumstances be eliminated without injury to investment. The elimination of profit would have to be attempted on a universal

* Edward Nell, 'Economics: the Revival of Political Economy', in Robin Blackburn (ed.), *Ideology in Social Science*, Fontana, 1972, p. 91.
† Ken Coates and Tony Topham (eds.), *Workers' Control*, p. 320.

scale. 'One had to attack the market over the whole front. If one did not, it remained unscathed, and quietly negatived all partial attacks that might be made on it.' * Such a universal effort to oust profit is unrealistic, as indeed is conceded by some Left-wing writers. 'For the foreseeable future at any rate, no formation of the Left will be in a position seriously to place the question of socialism on the agenda of most advanced capitalist societies.' †

The most that can be attempted in these circumstances is to reduce the rate of profit, particularly in high profit-earning sectors. This, however, requires a prices and incomes policy; the study of a hitherto neglected field – comparative rates of profit in different countries; and at the end of the day some co-ordination of policies internationally.

The second weakness of the Left's viewpoint is that it sees the social problem, and therefore the problem of inflation in so far as this is the product of social conditions, as exclusively one of conflict between labour and capital. It follows from Chapter One that the rivalry between labour and capital for shares in the national income does indeed contribute to inflation, but it has also been seen that this is by no means the whole of the issue. There are rival claims on increases in the national income between different groups of labour; these also contribute to inflation. 'The possibility of securing higher wages in the motor vehicle group than in the rest of engineering is largely due to the fact that output per man hour has been increasing far more rapidly in the motor vehicle sector ... Consequently, the high earnings in the fast growth motor vehicle group inspire conscientious shop-stewards in low growth and lower earning industrial groups to seek more money for their constituents and to reduce the 'unfair' differentials between comparable workers in the various groups.' ‡ The writings of the contemporary Left nowhere seek to deal with this problem of the ability of some workers to raise their pay

* Ken Coates and Tony Topham, *Workers' Control*, p. xxx.
† Ralph Miliband, *The State in Capitalist Society*, Weidenfeld and Nicolson, 1970, p. 275.
‡ Shirley Lerner and Judith Marquand, 'Regional Variations in Earnings, Demand for Labour, and Shop-Stewards' Combine Committees, in the British Engineering Industry' quoted in Ken Coates and Tony Topham (eds.), *Workers' Control*, pp. 214–15 and 217.

faster than others and the implications which this fact carries for the whole of society. It could be argued that competition between different groups of workers means that labour has taken on the colouring of the competitive capitalist environment. Even if capitalism and profit could be eliminated overnight, however, it would be unrealistic to expect the competitive psychology of labour instantly to change; it would linger on, and with it the problem of inflation. The abolition of capitalism and profit is, therefore, no answer to inflation; the answer lies in a recognition by both capital and labour that in fast-growing sectors there are limits to the extent to which they should pursue increases in profits and pay.

From the extreme or revolutionary Left let us turn to the 'reformist' or Social Democratic Left. The goals of the Social Democratic Left are no longer as clear cut as they were. They can no longer be summed up in the single word, 'Nationalization'. For nationalization, as we have seen, has not eliminated profit. Nor has it substituted a new set of managers or even a new style of management for the old. The prerogatives of management have remained practically untouched. It is possible that the 'reformist' Left may unfurl one of these days the banner of a greater say for workers in the running of industry, beginning with joint consultation, leading onwards to the sharing with managements of decision-making in certain areas and possibly ultimately to workers' control, with managers being elected by workers. Whatever merits this aim might have, it would not of itself, however, be a solution to inflation. It would still be open to workers commanding a leading sector to appropriate to themselves the whole of the growth of that sector, thus setting a pattern in pay increases causing tension and liable to be imitated elsewhere, with inflationary consequences. There would still be required, therefore, a rule limiting behaviour on incomes: Yugoslavia, which, as indicated in Chapter Five, has based its economic system on workers' control, has none the less had to introduce an incomes policy.

Meanwhile the current objective of the Social Democratic Left may be more modestly expressed: the eradication of poverty and inequality, including the 'infinitely harsher poverty of the

developing countries'. * The removal of poverty entails, however, the conquest of inflation, for rising prices, as we saw in Chapter One, bear most severely on the poor. And so we are back at rules of behaviour on incomes and prices – but incomes as well as prices. For 'The dividing-line between the "haves" and the "have-nots" no longer runs between the manual workers and the rest of the community: it follows a much more complex route. In terms of current income, many manual workers are to be found on the "haves" side of the barricade ... to pretend that resources can somehow be redistributed in favour of the poor at no cost to the majority, is to pave the way for de-moralization and disillusionment once the attack is launched.'†
The Social Democratic Left cannot escape the need for a com-pact on prices and incomes any more than can the revolutionary Left.

Finally we arrive at the extreme Right of the political spectrum. The Right is nowadays identified with the theory that the unlimited pursuit of self-interest conduces to the maximum interest of all. The theory may have something to it if the units in society are small. It loses validity, however, with the existence of units that are large. It can no longer be said that a wage settled by arbitra-tion is necessarily in the best interest of all; for it is not reached by impersonal market forces; it is a compromise arranged between two powerful groups. Nor, for similar reasons, can it be said that a price determined by one firm among three or four is necessarily in the best interest of all. The theory thus becomes subject to heavy qualification, possibly to the point of ruling it out as an explanation for many phenomena as well as a prescription for policy. Seen as history the theory has given rise to the pursuit of the maximum wage as well as the maximum profit, to the opposition of labour and capital, to the confrontation of classes, to the alternation of nationalization and denationalization, and the neglect of investment caused by the resulting uncertainty. And seen as philosophy the theory cuts clean across the basic requirement of society – namely, that I limit the pursuit of my

* Roy Jenkins, *What Matters Now*, Fontana, 1972, pp. 114–15.
† ibid. p. 117.

own interest out of regard for other people's interest, for only thus can we live together.

Indeed the theory is, paradoxically, at variance with the tenets of traditional conservatism. If the word conservatism has any content at all, it means a veneration for institutions inherited from the past. There is only one reason why legacies from the past should be venerated: because they embody the social compact; they are the cement that holds society together; and their preservation is the guarantee that the compact can be continued into the future. Nowhere is the contrast between contemporary theorizing on the Right and fundamental conservatism more vividly brought out than in Disraeli: 'These reflections lead me to a consideration of the great object of our new school of statesmen in general, which is to form political institutions on abstract principles of theoretic science, instead of permitting them to spring from the course of events, and to be naturally created by the necessities of nations. It would appear that this scheme originated in the fallacy of supposing that theories produce circumstances, whereas the very converse of the proposition is correct, and circumstances indeed produce theories ... They [the statesmen of the past] held themselves bound by the contracts of their forefathers, because they wished their posterity to observe their own agreements. They did not comprehend how the perpetuity of a State could be otherwise preserved. They looked upon the nation as a family, and upon the country as a landed inheritance.' *

It will be seen that the theories uttered from both ends of the political spectrum do not deal with the problem of price and wage leadership described in Chapter Two. The theory of the maximization of self-interest propounded from the extreme Right makes for price and wage leadership. The theory of the exploitation of labour by capital enunciated on the extreme Left takes no account of it. The only way of coping with the problem of wage and price leadership is to introduce or re-introduce into behaviour on prices and incomes the idea of a compact which both Right and Left accept as applicable to ordinary social behaviour. Admittedly, this is difficult. The individualism of the nineteenth

* Benjamin Disraeli, 'Vindication of the English Constitution', in *Whigs and Whiggism*, pp. 119 and 124.

century against which trade unions were originally a revolt may have reached the point where both firms and trade unions, or parts of trade unions, are intent only on maximizing their own immediate gain regardless of wider concerns, and that what we have is buccaneering private enterprise by firms and trade unions alike. To accept this situation, however, is to assume that there can be only a near horizon to men's thoughts, that men cannot see their interest in the longer as well as in the shorter term. After all, men still have to live in a society which is concerned with putting a brake on inflation. Inflation arises because of competitive claims on the increase in the national product. If each competitor, each section of labour or capital, pushes his claim to the bitter end, he will, through damaging society, ultimately damage himself. The purpose of the compact and of the non-partisan body whose function it is to act as custodian of the compact is to recall to each claimant the limits beyond which, in the interests of society and himself, he should not go.

Non-partisanship is not only required for the adjudication of conflicting claims on the increase in the national product as they are expressed in the industrial arena, it is also necessary for the continued competition of parties in the complementary political arena. Just as there are limits to the extent to which an industrial claimant can push his case, so also are there limits to the extent to which a political party can push its policies. A political party which presses its point too far can loosen the cohesiveness of society and so impair its ability to govern. Political partisanship cannot function without a background awareness of the need, on occasion, to be non-partisan.

Further, both conservatives and radicals have this in common – both are interested in the maintenance of the political system within which they function, whether it be a system of two or many parties. The system requires that the reigning party (or parties) submit itself (or themselves) after a period of time for electoral approval or rejection. As that moment approaches, the temptation to inflate, to expand the economy without incurring the full consequences of the expansion in rising prices, is considerable. We have seen that in the United Kingdom Governments of different political persuasion succumbed in turn to this temptation – a Conservative Government in 1959 and 1964, a nominally more radical Government in 1970. This is the Achilles heel of the democratic political system. If competition for votes between two or more parties is seen to be synonymous with inflation, to give rise to an increase in prices which arbitrarily redistributes incomes between different social groups, the resulting sense of injustice could develop to a point which would put the system in jeopardy.

One of two things might then happen. Competition for votes between two or more parties might give way to a soliciting for votes at periodic intervals by one party only. True, that one party would not be entirely insensitive to public opinion. It would also contain many differences of view and, therefore, many factions. The differences would, however, be concealed up to a point within one party. And the fact that it was one party searching for votes rather than two or more parties would imply a system different from that which countries with their political origins in Western Europe have hitherto known.

Alternatively democracy as known in the West or competition for votes between two or more parties might survive, but subject to an important condition – namely, that Governments could induce a state of well-being in the electorate at the approach of an election without at the same time, or at any rate shortly after, incurring severe inflation. This would be the preferable outcome, for at least two reasons. First, this is the system to which countries with political regimes modelled on Western Europe are accustomed, and countries should not lightly cast aside that to which they are accustomed. For 'a wise statesman will be careful that all new rights shall, as it were, spring from out old establishments. By this system alone can at the same time the old be purified and the new rendered permanent.' * Second, there is a presumption that Government is better when its doings are fully open to challenge by potential rivals than when they are half-concealed in one party.

The condition for realizing this second and preferable alternative is, however, onerous – an effective prices and incomes policy.

* Benjamin Disraeli, 'Vindication of the English Constitution', in *Whigs and Whiggism*, p. 140.

In other words, a Government must feel free to expand the economy without fearing that in so doing it will lose all control over prices and incomes. There has as yet been no *effective* prices and incomes policy in the United Kingdom; there have been essays at one, half-begun efforts cluttered with impedimenta from the past. It could be that effectiveness might mean the abandonment of some traditional economic freedom in order to preserve a larger political freedom. That choice is sufficiently stark to warrant at any rate a persistent attempt.

Chapter Twelve

The Shape of a Long-Term Policy

We have analysed inflation as arising from two sources: first, wage leadership, possibly originating in the fastest growing sectors because it is in these that power is most easily exercised, the leader in wage increases being then followed by others; second, price leadership, the signal flashed by the leader in the strongest position to do so again being followed by others. The imitativeness in wage and price increases is due partly to the imitativeness of human nature, partly to the quest for equity in a society in which all, nominally at any rate, enjoy political equality, the quest now being undertaken, not only by white against white, but also by coloured against white, and by women against men. This quest for equity in a society of political equals is characteristic of all modern societies and is likely to intensify rather than abate with time. It is thus both a universal and, as far as can be foreseen, a growing and therefore permanent problem. Its solution requires, therefore, a permanent policy. There can, on occasion, be a case for a 'freeze', for holding prices and incomes as they are, for three months as in the United States from August 15th, 1971, for six months as in the United Kingdom in the summer of 1966, or for something in between as in the United Kingdom in the autumn of 1972, but seldom for any longer interval than six months. What matters, however, is the overall policy for prices and incomes to be sought after emergence from the 'freeze' or from uniformity.

Let us first be clear as to what a prices and incomes policy cannot do. It cannot of itself do away with the basic antagonism of labour and capital, or the opposition, as seen by workers, between profits and wages. But it can be helped and complemented by measures designed to abate this antagonism and opposition. The antagonism could derive from the authoritarian nature of government in industry. Insofar as this is so, there could be greater participation by workers in certain aspects of industrial activity, on the lines, for example, of 'the rights of workmen's inspection given under Section 123 of the Mines Act; those are considerably in advance of the provisions of the Factories Acts so far as workers' participation and potential initiative on safety matters are concerned.' *

Or the opposition seen between profits and wages could stem from the fact that the ownership of capital is limited to a few. Insofar as this is so, a possible reconciliation between wages and profits might be found in a scheme whereby companies lodged part of their retained earnings in the name of their employees, in a capital fund managed, with the help of investment experts, by the T U C. The point of such a scheme is that it could facilitate the entry of workers into the possession of capital and, therefore, to a claim on profits generally – as distinct from the profits of one's own firm, as in the traditional profit-sharing scheme. It would give workers a share in stock exchange gains, such gains having an influence, neglected, as far as I can see in current economic writings, on wage claims. And it would remove the apparent anomaly that, whereas the wage-earner is subjected in any incomes policy to some limitation on the increase in his money income, the capital-owner is subjected to no limit in the appreciation of his capital. There are schemes either proposed or in being in various Western European countries. For example, all employers, private and public, could contribute to the fund proportionately to their wages bills. The assets in which the fund was invested could belong to all workers equally, so that an individual employee's entitlement would be equal to everybody else's. It is clear that a worker's share in the capital fund should not be immediately realizable, for this would aggravate the rate of inflation; it is equally clear that realization should be possible not later than the date of retirement. It is also fair to say that

* Ken Coates and Tony Topham (eds.), *Workers' Control*, Panther Modern Society, 1970, p. 382.

management would have to reconcile itself to the idea of share ownership by trade unions. *

Neither schemes for greater participation by workers nor for greater share-owning by workers will dispense, however, with the need for a prices and incomes policy; for such schemes try to deal mainly with the problem of labour versus capital, whereas there is, in addition, the problem of sector versus sector. 'The workers of pit, area, the whole mining industry, or the whole energy industry including oil, gas, electricity supply, etc. . . . how are the conflicting interests of these workers to be resolved?'† Through a prices and incomes policy which, however, gives rise to the following questions: How shall the rules be formulated and what shall they be? What shall be the institution or institutions for adjudicating whether the rules are being observed? How shall the rules be enforced? How shall the three functions of formulation, adjudication and enforcement be allocated so as to make for the effectiveness of the policy without at the same time heaping too much on any one organization?

We saw in Chapter Nine that in the United States the Administration laid down a broad aim for a reduction in the rate of inflation, leaving it to a Price Commission and a Pay Board to determine in detail how the aim should be achieved. In the United Kingdom, by contrast, both in 1966 and in 1972 the Government itself drew up all the rules. It is desirable, if possible, for the rules, both general and detailed, to be formulated through a parley between the Government, trade unions and managements. Nor is there anything unparliamentary in this procedure; the procedure does, however, recognize an inadequacy in contemporary Parliaments. In medieval England the monarch kept himself informed through a Parliament comprising the three 'estates of the realm' – the clergy, the wealthier nobles, and the lesser nobles or knights. With the growth of towns and the increasing weight of taxation falling on their richer inhabitants, representatives of the latter were fused with the knights to form a non-elected House of Commons or House of Squires. An 'estate of the realm'

* Aubrey Jones, 'A Policy for Prices and Incomes Now', *Lloyds Bank Review*, January 1972, pp. 5–6.

† Ken Coates and Tony Topham (eds.), *Workers' Control*, p. 420.

became a 'class established into a political order' so that: 'The great art in creating an efficient Representative Government is to secure its representation of those *interests* of the country which are at the same time not only considerable, but in their nature permanent.' * Those interests, or the modern counterparts of the ancient estates of the realm, are now Labour and Capital.

There has been a tendency in the post-war period for national assemblies specifically representative of 'interests' to reappear. For example, Holland has a Social and Economic Council, chaired by an independent chairman, and comprising representatives of the Government, employers and trade unions. The Council tenders to the Dutch Government advice on projected measures of a social or economic nature. Similarly, as we have seen, the United Kingdom has a National Economic Development Council, chaired, unlike its Dutch counterpart, by a Minister; it is served by a National Economic Development Office (NEDO) directed by an independent director – that is, by someone who is not a Government official. It is in such assemblies, or subcommittees of them, that a prices and incomes policy is best hammered out, with the independent chairman or independent director playing the role of mediator between the Government and the 'interests'. Where there is no such assembly a Government has to guess as best it can what will carry assent. An assembly of 'interests' is desirable because the rules have to appear fair; to appear fair they have to be demonstrated to be grounded in reason; the demonstration can emerge only through debate. For this purpose a forum is required.

Governments stemming from an elected forum tend to take a limited view of the discussion appropriate to a newer forum of 'interests'. Such a limited view proved to be a major cause of the failure of the United Kingdom Government in the autumn of 1972 to secure agreement on a voluntary policy. The trade unions were clearly interested in talking about the Industrial Relations Act and taxation. The Government regarded both as the prerogative solely of the elected forum. Formally the Government

* Benjamin Disraeli, 'Vindication of the English Constitution', 1835, reprinted in *Whigs and Whiggism: Political Writings by Benjamin Disraeli*, edited by William Hutcheon, John Murray, 1913, pp. 159 and 188.

was right; in substance it was seeking to separate issues which are inseparable. We showed in Chapter Eight that there is a close connection between 'industrial relations' and 'prices and incomes'. There is also a close connection between taxation and prices and incomes. The gross money income of manual workers in the United Kingdom rose between 1968 and 1970 at an annual rate of 10 per cent; in real terms this was equivalent to an annual increase of 3·6 per cent; when account was taken of extra taxation, however, the net real increase was only 1·3 per cent a year. Similarly in the United States the gross money income of manual workers between 1966 and 1970 rose at an annual rate of 4·7 per cent; in real terms this was equivalent to an annual increase of 0·8 per cent; after taking tax into account, however, there was no real increase – there was a decrease of 0·3 per cent a year. * Firms and trade unions necessarily, therefore, respond to such 'actions' of Governments as increased taxation; Governments have no alternative but to discuss these actions. To attain office Governments require a majority of individual votes; to govern effectively when office has been attained Governments need to carry with them the diverse interest groups.

It was the theme of Chapters Two, Three and Eleven that the individualist ideas inherited from the nineteenth century gave an inadequate view of how markets work and gave rise to inadequate prescriptions for dealing with the present-day problem of inflation. It was equally the theme of Chapter Eight that an undue emphasis on the individual versus the group could make more difficult the 'government' of industry. We are now seeing in the wider field of politics that institutions born of the same individualist tradition – for example, an elected assembly – need to be complemented by other institutions. The elected assembly is still the ultimate assembly for ratification and enactment; the assembly of 'interests', or some semblance of it, is that in which rules are best negotiated and in which Governments have to be readier to discuss the wider range of subjects which bear upon rules.

Governments, having played a crucial part in initiating the

* Dudley Jackson, H. A. Turner and Frank Wilkinson, *Do Trade Unions Cause Inflation?*, Cambridge University Press, 1972, pp. 66 and 102.

formulation of the rules, have then to decide what role they play in saying whether or not the rules are being observed. We gave reasons in the last chapter why the task of adjudicating whether or not particular price and incomes decisions or proposals were in conformity with the rules should be entrusted to an independent non-partisan body. Assuming there to be such a body, Governments have to decide whether or not they pick and choose cases to refer to it, whether, that is to say, they retain a discretionary power, or whether they allow it a comprehensive scope.

We have seen that in the matter of strikes entailing a public 'emergency', political authority in the United Kingdom has retained a greater discretionary power than its counterparts in either the United States or Canada. We saw that in the United States the Administration cannot act without first establishing a fact-finding body, though the latter has no power to make recommendations. In Canada there was a more extreme suggestion: that an Independent Industrial Relations Commission should recommend what should be done in the case of such strikes. In the United Kingdom, by contrast, a Government has only to indicate to the judiciary that in its view an emergency exists. Thus in 1972 a Conservative Government applied on this ground to the National Industrial Relations Court for a ballot of railway workers as to whether or not a rail strike should be 'allowed' to continue. In so doing the Government aggravated the suspicion already incurred of being against the trade unions in all its doings and for the time being worsened its prospects of reaching agreement with the trade unions on criteria for incomes and prices.

In the matter of prices and incomes the contrast between the United Kingdom, on the one hand, and the United States and Canada, on the other, has been equally striking. In the United Kingdom between 1965 and 1970 the Government picked and chose its references to the Prices and Incomes Board as it wished, thus playing the primary role in the act of adjudication. In the United States, on the other hand, from November 1971 onwards, the Pay Board and the Price Commission dealt comprehensively with all cases, determining their methods as they thought fit. And in Canada the Prices and Incomes Commission, while receiving references from the Government, usually chose its own references.

The case against the retention of all discretionary power by the Government is conclusive. It is that an elected Government can often put its own party interest above the public interest and can certainly be under suspicion of doing so. The health of an elected system of Government depends on allaying, if not removing, that suspicion. The objection, on the other hand, to giving comprehensive scope to a non-partisan body is that it could become a body of inordinate size. How can its size be contained? The answer depends in part on the tasks entrusted to the organization and the manner in which it is required to approach its task.

It was stated earlier that in the United Kingdom in 1970 the then Labour Government proposed the establishment of a Commission for Industry and Manpower which would include, among other organizations, the existing Monopolies Commission. There is clearly a connection between the monopolistic structure of industry and prices. To limit, however, the size of an adjudicating body on prices, problems of industrial structure could still be left to a Monopolies Commission. More important is the connection between industrial relations, on the one hand, and prices and incomes, on the other. Both are concerned with the struggle for shares of the national income; further, the conciliatory approach to industrial relations can set a precedent for an approach to prices and incomes. In no country that I know of, certainly not in the United States or in the United Kingdom, has an attempt been made to dovetail together these two subjects or the different bits and pieces of legislation governing them, owing their origin as they do to different moments of history and to different intellectual backgrounds. It is this amalgamation that should now be attempted.

I have described how, until recently, Government regarded its function in regard to collective bargaining as that of holding the ring between contestants of supposedly equal bargaining power. To discharge this task it created, at any rate in the United Kingdom, a network of some sixty referees, known as a conciliation service. The time has arrived when the Government is interested, not just in holding the ring, but in the outcome of the contest.

As a result the neutrality of a Government has come into question. As the referee in industrial relations the position of a Government has now been undermined. In the United Kingdom employers and trade unions have begun to establish their own rudimentary conciliation service, with the Government still retaining its own main network. A conciliation service set up by employers and trade unions alone could be dangerous, for it could ignore the interest of the consumer or the interest of society in the outcome of the contest. The logical answer to a situation in which faith has been lost in the Government conciliation service, must be the constitution of an organization independent of the Government of the day concerned certainly with strikes, but also with inflation.

Hitherto these two subjects have been treated separately. In the United Kingdom the Governmental conciliation service has pursued before all else the objective of avoiding strikes, with only secondary attention to the objective of avoiding inflationary settlements. On the other hand, a body such as the Prices and Incomes Board was concerned primarily with the avoidance of inflationary settlements and was not formally required to pay regard to the avoidance of strikes. Since both objectives are of importance to the national economy and since the pursuit of one can be at the expense of the other, it follows that the attainment of the two should be sought under the guidance of the same body.

Suppose this guiding body is the Prices and Incomes Board. We may as well call it that, for the camouflage of any other name or names is only too easily seen through. The Board should comprise a nucleus of independent members, with additional members drawn from management and unions and retaining their footing in those fields. It would have to deal with two quite different attitudes – the older attitude of unions and employers in looking to the Government for help in composing their differences and the newer attitude of Government towards the size of the settlement. It was seen in Chapter Eight that it took several decades to secure acceptance of the principle of Government mediation in industrial disputes. And it would be unrealistic to expect overnight acceptance of the Government's interest in the outcome of an industrial contest. It would be the task of the Board to effect a bridge between the old and the new, to use the older methods of persuasion but in the cause of the newer interest in abating inflation. We shall be in a better position to see how it might proceed when we have considered the rules which might be laid down for it.

They should meet certain requisites: they should have an economic foundation; they should be fair in the sense that nobody in principle could take exception to them; they should be symmetrical between prices and incomes, for these are different faces of the same distributive coin; and they should be such as not to bring upon the adjudicator too large an administrative load.

There can be no disagreement over the economic logic – the average increase in wages ought not to exceed the prospective rate of increase in the gross domestic product per employee, for this is a necessary, though not sufficient, condition to ensure the stability of prices. The further condition is that in sectors where the rate of increase in output per employee is faster than the average, the difference must be reflected in reduced prices, and not just taken out in extra profit. There clearly could be disagreement over what the rate of increase in the gross domestic product could be, the trade unions generally contending that it could be higher than the Government's forecast. Any such disagreement would have to be resolved within the forum of 'interests'. Let it only be noted that the Government will not be in a position to guarantee that its forecast will be realized; in other words, it will not necessarily be able to 'deliver the goods'.

The greater disagreement is likely to arise over the manner and possibly the extent of the weight which should be given to equity. It is a sense of inequity which can give rise to strikes. And inequity or a sense of it both causes and results from inflation. It is right, therefore, that the rules should in some degree take into account inflation; but preferably past rather than future inflation, for the fuller the account taken of possible future inflation the more certain is it that that fact will itself bring inflation about.

Inflation accelerates as each group in society comes to accept it as a fact of life and takes steps to protect itself against it – by, for example, linking its income to the rate of increase in prices. The more complete the protection throughout society, the faster the pace of inflation. A reduction in the pace requires that the protection be limited. What is needed, therefore, is a minimal but acceptable principle of protection. How does one reach a (fair) principle? By asking a simple question: Which groups in society would be accepted most as deserving of continued protection against inflation at least for some time to come? Surely two: the relatively poorest and those whose pay had lagged behind the most in the preceding inflation.

The relatively poorest could be defined only arbitrarily. Let us suppose it is agreed that they are those in the lowest quartile in the earnings league. In the United Kingdom in April 1972 they would have been those men earning around £27 per week. To keep their income in line with rising prices would have required a pay increase somewhat above the economically desirable figure; how far above would depend on the pace of the preceding inflation. The strict economic standard can thus be explicitly tempered by a consideration for equity. As the inflation was brought under control the definition of the relatively poorest could be amended to, say, the lowest decile.*

Let us not, however, exaggerate the extent to which a prices and incomes policy can help the low paid. We saw in Chapter Five how, when the pay of the relatively poor was raised, the mountain of pay differentials above them rose still higher. We have to think of instruments additional to a prices and incomes policy to assist the low paid: help through taxes according to the size of families, the establishment of industry in depressed areas, and, above all, the maintenance of full employment.

* In the autumn of 1972 the British Government put forward a proposal which would have married the economically desirable figure with a socially equitable figure. The proposal was for a flat pay increase of £2 per week. In percentage terms this would have meant a bigger increase for the lower paid than for the higher paid. On average it would have implied a percentage increase roughly equal to the prospective increase in the national product per employee. As a short-term measure it was a useful device. But in the longer term it would have narrowed differentials unrealistically. It would not, therefore, have stood the test of time.

As for those whose pay settlements are reached at longish intervals, their problem can be dealt with by making it clear that the standard percentage increase in pay is related to one year. Those who last had a pay increase more than a year previously could be entitled to an addition to the standard figure for an increase, the addition being determined at a rate of so much for each month over and above the year. Correspondingly those who last had a pay increase less than a year ago could suffer a deduction from their standard increase, the amount being arrived at in the same way.* A clear statement that the percentage pay increase was related to one year would mean that those who had a pay increase on the eve of a policy would not, therefore, enjoy an unfair advantage relative to others.

The policy then would deal with inequities arising from differences in the timing of pay settlements, as well as from differences in current levels of pay. These, of course, are not the only inequities. There is also the inequity felt by those who see their pay fall behind pay received by others for what they regard as similar work. As indicated in Chapter Five, the only long-term method of meeting this particular sense of inequity is to develop techniques for measuring as objectively as possible the contents of jobs. The development of such techniques will, however, be a long uphill task. While they are being evolved the policy will be under considerable strain from this particular source of felt 'unfairness'. And even when they are evolved they will not ensure that emulative pay increases are done away with; they should, however, lessen the scope for loose comparison and help show that some comparisons are less valid than others.

Finally, there is the inequity felt by those who are not paid according to results and who cannot, therefore, couch their pay claim on grounds of a contribution to increased productivity. As stated in Chapter Five, there should be no room in a long-term policy for unlimited pay increases in the name of productivity, as there was in Britain between 1965 and 1970, for the simple reason that the source of the increase in productivity is frequently impossible to identify. Systems of payment by results

---

* *See* Aubrey Jones, "How I would run the incomes policy', *Sunday Times*, 5 November 1972, p. 16.

are likely to be with us, however, for a long time to come because of the prevalence of the belief that money is an incentive to effort, though the areas covered by them could probably be narrowed without adverse consequences. So long as they are there a sense of inequity will be bred in the breasts of adjacent workers paid according to time rather than according to results. This sense of inequity must needs be met; and the fact of meeting it will mean a further unspecified addition to the economically desirable rate of increase in pay. But any such increase in pay ought to be taken account of when considering other shorter-term increases.

We have so far dealt with the basic rules for incomes. We now come to the rules for prices. These too should come under the guidance of the Prices and Incomes Board. We saw that the Board set up in the United Kingdom in 1965 was originally envisaged as having two divisions: a Prices Division and an Incomes Division. This separation was never in practice observed. The United States Administration none the less, while drawing many lessons from the British experience, established two distinct bodies: a Price Commission and a Pay Board. While the British did many things that were mistaken between 1965 and 1970, they were right in treating prices and incomes together. A prices and incomes policy deals with specific cases. In each specific case it is desirable to trace through time the chain effect of a pay increase on prices and of a price or profit increase on pay. It is desirable for the management members of one and the same Board to see and to assume responsibility for the consequences for pay of a decision on prices and profits; and for the trade union members to see and assume responsibility for the consequences on prices of a decision on pay.

Further, the rules for prices are derived as a corollary to the rules for incomes. Let us suppose that the rules for increases in incomes so work out that they provide for an average annual increase of 6 per cent; and that the annual rate of increase in the gross domestic product is 4 per cent per employee. Then the broad rule for increases in prices will be 2 per cent a year – the difference, that is, between the rate of increase in the product per employee and the average increase in incomes. Some firms would need to raise their prices by more than this, either because the rate of increase in productivity per employee was low but they were required nonetheless to pay a 'fair' wage increase; or because of a concentration of low-paid workers, a circumstance that generally goes together with a low rate of increase in productivity. Other firms with a rapid rate of increase in productivity would have to decrease their prices by as much as the rule: price reductions are for management the necessary counterpart to wage restraint by trade unions. The Board should concentrate in the first instance on those who claimed a price increase greater than that provided for in the rules. As time went on it would be necessary for it, though very difficult, to transfer its attention more to those who were to reduce their prices as provided for in the rules. It would have to work out its own indicators of the movement in productivity in different sectors, so that it would have a sound idea of which sectors were reasonably entitled to price increases and which could afford to decrease their prices. The same information would also be valuable for the Board's work on wages.

Rules for prices derived in this way from rules for pay assume an unchanged average rate of profit or an unchanged ratio of profits to investment. Since a prices and incomes policy is related to all forms of income we need a rule for profits. We saw in Chapter Six that it is impossible to determine what is a 'proper' rate of profit. The nearest the British Prices and Incomes Board got to an objective measurement of profit was through a comparison of the prospective return on an investment with the cost of the needed capital. This comparison could not be applied to many cases. The question of comparative rates of profit in different countries requires much deeper study; it is very pertinent to economic policy-making in, for example, a European Economic Community. In default of a measure of the 'proper' rate of profit, we had better take a leaf out of the American book and speak of the profit margin – that is, the ratio of profits to sales. The use of this expression has the advantage that, when an economy is expanding, which is the time when a prices and incomes policy is most needed, sales should be increasing; the ratio of profits to sales could therefore remain unchanged, and yet profits could be growing, thus providing funds for investment. It was seen in Chapter Nine that in the United States firms are required not to increase prices if profit margins are raised above the average of the best two of the last three years. A broad rule could therefore be that a firm would be required to show why it wished to increase its profit margin.

Not all claims for increases in pay, prices or profit margins need be notified. It was seen in Chapter Nine that in the United States prior notification before approval was required for pay claims affecting some 10 per cent of the working force and for prices affecting some 45 per cent of sales. Spot checks were undertaken to ensure that where approval was not required the rules were none the less observed. If the suggested Prices and Incomes Board is to be the sole adjudicator and is not to share adjudication with the Government, as was the case in the United Kingdom between 1964 and 1970, then notification should be to the Board, not to the Government. On receipt of a claim for either a wage or a price/profit increase which appears well outside the rules the Prices and Incomes Board should proceed to act in the spirit of conciliation, for, it was argued earlier, it is necessary to erect a bridge between the methods of dealing with the older form of the dispute over shares in the national income – industrial relations – and the newer form – prices and incomes. It should not stand passively by, waiting for the claim to take effect; nor should it defer action until the matter had been referred to it by the Government. It should offer its assistance to the parties to meet the rules. It should actively intervene, the level of authority at which the intervention is undertaken being dependent on the importance of the claim. Throughout, the Board should endeavour to persuade. To this end it would be helpful if there were transferred to it the present Government conciliation service numbering some sixty officials. Their task would not be to conciliate between the two sides, as of old, but to persuade both sides to accept the rules. A comparable body of conciliators would be required for prices.

If, despite the assistance offered, the parties should reach, or be in danger of reaching, a pay settlement or pushing through a price increase judged by the Board, in the light of the rules, to be unjustifiably high, the Board should publish its own view of what the outcome should be, setting out its reasons. This view could, as in Australian legislation, be described as an 'award'. The 'award' could be accepted. Equally it could be rejected: if it were a matter of pay, the union could defy it and go on strike; if it were a matter of price, the firm could defy it. The Board could again intercede and discuss its 'award' with both parties. But if it is still unable to elicit what would in its view be a reasonable response, what then? Should everything stop there? Or, persuasion exhausted, should the policy include recourse to a sanction?

The case for 'voluntarism' is that men are not automata; they will comply provided they see reason why they should comply; their response will change as their understanding is enlarged. Thus interpreted, 'voluntarism' shows a deeper knowledge of human nature than the view that men react unvaryingly to changes in the level of unemployment or in the supply of money. Even so, the knowledge is not deep enough. However much the understanding expands, the problem expands too; and the chances are that understanding will always lag behind the problem. The problem of inflation is here now; it threatens us with serious consequences and this gulf between problem and understanding in the present has twice given rise to sanctions in the United Kingdom – 1966 and 1972, and once in the United States – 1971. We cannot, therefore, without closer scrutiny dismiss the case for sanctions in the longer term.

Sanctions are widely applied against individuals when their behaviour places at risk the welfare of other individuals or of the whole society of which they are members. The objection to sanctions on prices and incomes can scarcely be based on the ground that the economic interest of the individual automatically coincides with that of society. We have seen that it does not. Economic behaviour does not, therefore, differ from any other kind of behaviour. But an objection to certain sanctions on prices and incomes can be justifiably grounded in impracticability. To apply a sanction against every price and income contract which breached the rules would scarcely be feasible, any more than it is feasible against every breach of the highway code. Nor can sanctions be symmetrical as between prices and incomes. For prices are determined by firms, and the firms that matter are not all that numerous. Incomes, on the other hand, are received by masses of people, and masses cannot be punished. They can recognize a moral authority, and the authority can be supported by a sanction; but without the prior recognition the sanction cannot prevail.

It is a matter of individual judgement as to whether or not a policy would command moral assent, and a matter of practice as to whether or not a Prices and Incomes Board would command moral authority, so that the rules prevailed primarily through persuasion and recourse to a sanction was a rarity. It is my belief, however, that for the longer term a sanction is required. Every policy will undergo its rhythm of relaxation and tightening. If, in the moment of relaxation, the policy is not to risk collapse, a sanction is needed. The appropriate sanction against a trade union striking in breach of the Board's 'award' would be a fine, but not disproportionately large in relation to the union's funds. We have to consider, however, not only trade unions as a formally organized body of workers, such as the United Automobile Workers Union of the United States and the Amalgamated Engineering Workers Union of the United Kingdom, but also informally assembled groups, possibly coming together for a particular purpose and dissolving again. In the United Kingdom they would normally be led by a shop steward and they would not necessarily be amenable to instruction or persuasion from a union proper. Such a grouping could equally defy an award of the Board by going on strike. The procedure to be applied could be exactly the same as in the case of defiance by a formal union – that is, persuasion first, with a possible culmination in a sanction. The ultimate sanction would, however, have to be different. Since the organization was not formal it could not be fined. Perhaps the farthest one could go would be to fine the leaders of the grouping provided they could be identified, the fine being collected if need be through a deduction from future earnings. There would be less of a problem in enforcing a price ruling against a firm; after persuasion had failed a fine could be levied in the same way.

A system of sanctions based on the criterion of practicability and, therefore, not capable of being applied symmetrically to firms and trade unions inevitably has loopholes. That is why it is important that the Board should throughout endeavour to persuade. The emphasis on persuasion would be in keeping with the purpose of the policy, which is to abate the tensions which can arise from too large differences in the rates of increase in pay and profits, not create new tensions. The procedure outlined is voluntary in all stages, until the end, when a sanction could be invoked.

But who should invoke it? Clearly not the 'conciliators', for if it were known that they were going to seek a sanction, they would seldom succeed in persuading. A distinction could possibly be drawn, as in the Australian Conciliation and Arbitration Commission, between two wings of the Prices and Incomes Board: a 'conciliation' wing, concentrating on persuasion, and an 'arbitration' wing consisting of different people, seeking to apply the sanction when persuasion had failed. But this would initially give the Prices and Incomes Board a confused image.

The recourse to a sanction should surely be by the Government. Faced with the breach of a Board's 'award', it should go to a High Court for the application of the appropriate fine. The Government would thus have played the initial role of formulating the rules, preferably in agreement with managements and trade unions; it would have left the intermediate role of adjudication or guidance to an independent body, the Prices and Incomes Board; and, if need be, it would reappear to seek the enforcement of the Board's awards. This would be in keeping with practice in the United States where enforcement is left to the Cost of Living Council. True, a Government could choose not to enforce; it could run away on the eve of an election; and the policy could collapse as it did in the United Kingdom in 1970. Government by popular election cannot, however, be entirely saved from its weaknesses. The most that can be attempted is some mitigation of them.

We have in this chapter already departed far from British practice in placing the entire act of adjudication with an independent body. Have we gone too far? I think not. We have traced inflation to a basic cause: a struggle for the division of current income between some workers and others, or between pay in general and profits, this struggle taking place no matter what the level of aggregate demand, whether this be high or low.

To deal with this cause there is required a set of rules governing both pay and prices (that is, profits) that in broad principle commands assent, and in the formulation of which the Government must play a part. To adjudicate whether or not the rules are being adhered to, or to guide parties in keeping to the rules, the Government has to seek a body outside itself, the Government resuming action on receipt of the adjudication. The reasons why the Government must seek an independent organization were set out in Chapter Ten, the main reason being that Governments drawn from political parties loosely associated with labour or capital are suspect in the struggle for shares in the national income. To create a 'non-partisan' body is not, therefore, to derogate from the rights of popularly elected Governments. It is to aim at fulfilling a function which modern Governments cannot by their nature discharge.

We have seen that popularly elected Governments bring about a political cycle which in turn determines the economic cycle. On advent to office they see an inflation which they fear may escalate beyond control. They clamp down on Government spending and restrict the supply of money. The result is higher unemployment with continued, if not worsened, inflation. As a new election approaches they are fearful in turn of the electoral effects of unemployment. They expand Government spending and the supply of money. The first half of their tenure thus consists largely of 'stop', induced by the fiscal and monetary restriction; the second consists largely of 'go', brought about by fiscal and monetary expansion. This description is broadly true of political systems in which two or more parties compete for electoral favour; and it may be true of systems with only one party within which, however, two or more factions may be struggling for power.

Now if, on attaining office, a Government were able to keep expansion going while still keeping inflation under control through an *effective* prices and incomes policy, it would not need to resort to fiscal and monetary restriction. Nor would it need, as another election loomed on the horizon, to indulge once again in an exaggerated expansion, for it would not have gone through a preliminary restriction. Clearly we are far from that point yet; a prices and incomes policy has first to be developed to the stage of effectiveness. The prize attending effectiveness is, however, great. In human terms it is the mitigation of the misery and waste of talent associated with the 'stop-go' cycle, the primary origin of which is political. Politically it is the continued existence of the competitive party system. In that case a Prices and Incomes Board, acting as the adjudicator and the guide to help ensure that the rules governing the determination of pay and profits are observed, does not threaten democracy as we know it; it becomes the permanent 'non-partisan' reminder that even in party politics there are limits beyond which partisanship should not be pushed; it is thus one of the keys to democracy's survival.

Postscript

Since this book was finished – early January 1973 – two developments of significance have taken place. First, the policy of the United States Administration which was described in Chapter Nine and which was based on earlier British and Canadian experience, moved into a new phase. Second, the United Kingdom Government, which, after the collapse of an attempt to introduce a voluntary policy, had 'frozen' all prices and incomes in November 1972, announced its intention to shift to a policy modelled on that of the United States, but without knowing that the United States Administration was about to change it.

The rules for wage and price increases laid down in the United States in November 1971 provided for an annual pay increase of $5\frac{1}{2}$ per cent a year (with exceptions on restricted grounds not exceeding 7 per cent a year) and for average prices increases of 'no more than $2\frac{1}{2}$ per cent per year', with the further limit that profit margins (that is, the ratio of profits to sales) should not exceed the company's experience in the best two of the three previous financial years. These rules were designed roughly to preserve the relative shares of the national income going to wages and profits, with some provision for an increase in the share of profits such as ordinarily accrues when business is recovering from a recession. The changes introduced in January 1973, and labelled 'Phase Three', left unaffected the broad rule for pay increases: $5\frac{1}{2}$ per cent a year, but modified the rules relating to price increases from $2\frac{1}{2}$ to $1\frac{1}{2}$ per cent, at the same time enabling a company, provided it observed the $1\frac{1}{2}$ per cent, to widen its profit margin; it could now aim at a profit margin equivalent to the average of the best two of the four (rather than three) preceding financial years. Companies thus appeared to be placed in a position in which, in exchange for a lower ceiling to price increases, they had greater room to raise profits.

More important, however, than the changes in the rules was the change effected in the institutions and in the policing arrangements. It was described in Chapter Nine how there had been established three institutions: a Cost of Living Council, consisting of Government officials, and charged with the task of determining broad objectives and enforcing the policy; a Price Commission, consisting of 'public members' only; and a Pay Board with initially equal representation of business, labour, and the public, but from which most of the trade-union representatives later withdrew. Under Phase Three the Price Commission and the Pay Board were abolished; portions of their staffs were transferred to the Cost of Living Council to supervise both pay and prices. This last move goes some way to meet the argument that the creation of two distinct bodies for prices and incomes was a mistake (p. 199). The abolition of the Price Commission and the Pay Board followed in part on a relaxation of the policing arrangements. Except for certain special sectors the requirement to notify intended price or wage increases and to secure approval before putting them into effect was ended. Industry was to be trusted to observe the rules of price and wage behaviour, but the Cost of Living Council was given authority to block violations if it had prior knowledge of them and to 'roll back' increases in excess of the rules after the event; violations were also retrospectively punishable with fines. While sanctions were thus retained in the background, the policy was considerably loosened, and this at a time when business was expanding and orthodox theory would expect price and wage increases to accelerate. Why?

The main clue to the answer is probably to be found in the readiness of the trade unions once more to cooperate with the Government. They agreed to play their part in a ten-man labour–management committee to advise the Cost of Living Council on whether the rules on pay should be changed and, if so, how. It has been a theme of this book that the rules on pay and those on prices are inextricably intertwined, and that the trade unions must therefore play their part in the determination of both. Be that as it may, the loosening of the policy coincided with the expression of a willingness by the trade unions to cooperate in drawing up rules on pay. There is a close parallel here with the British situation of 1962 (described on pp. 50–51). The British trade unions agreed to serve on the new National Economic Development Council, but almost simultaneously Mr Selwyn Lloyd's 'wage pause' was terminated. It may be that a policy, however 'tight', which is started without trade-union cooperation, has subsequently to be relaxed in order to secure it. At any rate, this evolution has now occurred twice within a decade, and on both sides of the Atlantic. Both episodes reinforce the need to obtain trade-union cooperation from the outset, if preceding policies allow it indeed to be obtained.

From the American Phase Three let us turn to the British post-'freeze' phase, which has been labelled the 'Second Stage' and enunciated in the same month as the American Phase Three. (The contents of Stage Two may undergo amendment as the required legislation passes through Parliament, and any comments made in this postscript may need subsequent qualification in the light of this possibility.) Let us look first at some of the details of the programme before considering the overall policy.

The rules governing behaviour in incomes and prices are to be set out in a more detailed Code which has not yet been formulated. The broad rule is that pay increases for any group of employees should be at annual intervals only and the yearly aggregate rise for the group 'should not exceed the sum which would result from the payment of £1 a week per head plus 4 per cent of the current pay bill [excluding overtime] for the group'. The rule is thus a combination of a flat pay increase and a percentage increase. In the autumn of 1972 the British Government had put forward a proposal for a simple flat pay increase of £2, but this device, while useful as a short-term measure, would not have stood the test of time in that it would have narrowed differentials to an unacceptable degree (p. 197); even in the short term the device would not have been acceptable to some unions because of the marked effect on differentials (see the quotation from the T U C's *Economic Review* for 1968 on p. 81).

The new combination of a flat-rate pay increase with a percentage increase means that the increases expressed in percentage

terms taper off the higher the absolute level of pay (a result which
the Prices and Incomes Board of 1965–70 sought to bring about
in its earlier days: see Allan Fels, *The British Prices and Incomes
Board*, p. 131).

The following table, constructed from the latest available
figures for the distribution of earnings in 1972 gives some indication of the 'taper':

Estimated effect of Stage 2 on increases in earnings*

Permitted wage increase in:	Lowest 10% of income earners	Lowest 25% of income earners	50% of income earners	Highest 25% of income earners	Highest 10% of income earners
£ per week	1·9	2·0	2·3	2·7	3·1
per cent	8·7	7·8	7·1	6·4	5·9

If it is assumed that appropriate tax concessions are made so
that rises in pay are not unduly affected by an increasing marginal
tax 'bite', then it will be seen that a cost of living increase of 7 per
cent will entail rises in real earnings for only 50 per cent of those
earning incomes from employment; a cost of living increase of 6
per cent will entail increases in real earnings for 75 per cent; and a
cost of living increase of 5½ per cent will mean increases in real
earnings for 90 per cent of income earners. As stated, the figures
for increases in earnings do not allow for the effect of 'wage drift',
the difference between the increase in negotiated wage rates and
the increase in actual earnings, which may arise from various
causes (both legitimate and illegitimate) and which may add as
much as two percentage points to the rates of wage increase.
However, the effect of wage drift is somewhat uneven, and therefore the Government should not rely upon this as a factor for
maintaining real earnings. We have seen throughout the book
that people are concerned with their real earnings. If most people
are not to have their real earnings reduced under the new policy,

*Adult male employees only, with approximate adjustments to exclude
overtime pay and to bring the data up to October 1972 (seasonally adjusted);
the figures given do not allow for 'wage drift'.

the rate of increase in prices (which was 7·1 per cent in 1972) has to be reduced by over one fifth. What are the chances of achieving such a reduction? To attempt an answer to this question, we need to look at the rules for prices, insofar as they are at present known.

These do *not* contain a standard for price increases, as did Phase Two in the United States, but some indication is given of the costs which manufacturers may take into account in determining prices, as well as an indication of target profit margins. Unavoidable cost increases – such as, for example, increases in the prices of imported raw materials – may be passed on in increased prices. So may increased labour costs in so far as they comply with the rules for pay, but not if they exceed them – which was precisely the case in the United Kingdom between 1965 and 1970. A reduction is to be made from allowable costs 'to ensure that the benefits of increased productivity are used to keep prices down'. This phrase presumably means that if a group of low-paid workers receive a justifiable pay increase of 8·7 per cent, and their productivity is rising at the rate of 2 per cent a year, the allowable labour-cost increase will be 6·7 per cent. To work out precisely the rate of increase in the productivity of a particular working group so as to determine how much of its extra pay may be passed on in prices is going to prove a difficult and complicated task. This is obvious from the experience of the Prices and Incomes Board: to assess productivity movements at the level of the enterprise, and even more so at the level of a working group, requires an expert investigatory body, but, as we shall see, it is doubtful whether the agencies established to enforce the policy will be able to act in this way.

What, finally, about the increases in costs inherited from the past? The White Paper notes that 'before the standstill ... increases in both wage rates and earnings were running at 15–16 per cent above a year before'. This, as we have seen, is one of the crucial problems that arise either on the inception of a policy or at a change of phase in a policy and is presumably to be met by the rule relating to profit margins which are not to be allowed to 'exceed the average level of the best two of the previous five years'.

What conclusions can one draw from these rules about the ability of the Government at least to maintain the real earnings of most of the population during Stage Two – for on this more than on anything else will the success of the policy depend? Success is not unattainable, the difference between the rate of increase in prices before the freeze (7 to 8 per cent a year) and the rate of increase necessary to maintain real earnings for most ($5\frac{1}{2}$ per cent) not being all that great. On the other hand, since wage increases in accordance with the pay rules will be an 'allowable cost', they are likely to raise prices by about 5 per cent. This leaves only a very narrow margin – $\frac{1}{2}$ a per cent – for other cost increases if prices are to be restrained to the extent necessary to ensure the success of the policy. True, the margin would be enlarged if deductions were made from increased labour costs on account of increases in productivity, but to measure these latter increases accurately is a difficult task requiring appropriate institutional machinery.

This machinery is to comprise a Price Commission and a Pay Board. The titles are copied from the United States and the functions of the two bodies are very much those that were exercised by the American bodies. In other words, notification of intended pay and price increases is to be direct to the relevant agencies, and in the case of 'larger' firms the prior approval of the Price Commission is required before price increases are put into effect. This aspect of the proposals is in keeping with the policy suggested in Chapter Twelve.

It seems as though the two agencies are to function in a quasi-judicial manner. A schedule to the Draft Bill, for example, indicates that an agency may hold inquiries, may examine witnesses under oath. We saw in the case of the Prices and Incomes Board that parties to the issue often did not know the true facts; to ascertain these and other relevant information on which to base a judgement studies had to be undertaken in the field: that is, outside the formal framework of an inquiry. The policy needs an investigatory body functioning in the way that the Prices and Incomes Board did, for many detailed issues will have to be decided (not only the extent of any increase in productivity but also such questions as the true amount of the 'current pay bill for the group, exclusive of overtime'). Both agencies will in fact be concerned with productivity: the Price Commission when considering pay increases for the purpose of determining 'allowable costs', and the Pay Board when considering increases in earnings under schemes of payment according to results. Their functions will therefore overlap, while the relevant expertise, insofar as it is obtainable consistently with the quasi-legalistic approach, will be divided between them.

The problem of separation between the two agencies while their functions in part overlap is made worse by the ostensible absence of any coordinating board analogous to the American Cost of Living Council. Although the Treasury is to draw up a common set of rules (*after* consultation but, significantly, not *in* consultation) with interested parties, there is to be no coordination of the policies of the two agencies in securing observance of the rules. Perhaps the Government has already conceded this argument in a singular clause of the Draft Bill to the effect that the Price Commission and the Pay Board may be amalgamated into a single agency. If when it comes to Stage Three the United Kingdom were again to follow the United States and bring prices and incomes policies sensibly together, a unified body will inevitably have to be created (to be called the Prices and Incomes Board?).

For all the apparent similarity between the new British Price Commission and Pay Board on the one hand, and their now defunct American counterparts on the other, there is one extremely important difference. It was noted in Chapter Eight that both in industrial relations and in prices and incomes Government in the United Kingdom tended to retain a greater discretionary power than did Governments in the United States and Canada. This tendency is still present in the proposals put forward for Stage Two, for 'Ministers will be able in exceptional circumstances and after consultation with the agency to approve increases not authorised by the agency'. The door is left open therefore for Ministers to allow a wage increase disapproved of by the Pay Board because they are fearful of a strike, or to allow a price increase not considered justifiable by the Price Commission because they are under pressure from a powerful firm. The path is there for a re-emergence of the contradictions described at length in Chapter Seven.

Thus the policies and institutions for Stage Two contain both actual and potential contradictions. Since they are 'imposed', they also violate an essential condition for eventual success – namely acceptability through agreed rules expressing 'the public interest' and in the light of which an independent agency adjudicates on particular cases. This may be an inevitable initial handicap of the policy; but what are the longer-term prospects?

Consider the thesis of this book: rising prices are no longer a temporary economic difficulty; for many years the new inflation has been the product of social responses to economic forces; more recently the new inflation has been paradoxically accelerated by social reactions against the 'traditional' attempts by the Government to deal with it. These responses and reactions arise inevitably in societies with high social and economic aspirations, so that the new inflation is thus both a developing and an enduring problem for modern economies.

A policy which is successfully to cope with inflation must therefore try to meet the relevant political and social forces. This means that it must be acceptable to the majority and this it can do only if it is fair, both in its rules and its operation.

It is thus important that the Government's own actions do not exacerbate the situation, and this point is recognized in the White Paper. Explicit measures are to be taken to mitigate the general effect on prices of the introduction of the Value Added Tax; an attempt is to be made to meet the problem of the increase in local authority rents and to soften the effect on the lower paid of a transition to more 'economic' rents; and further concessions may have been given to the lower paid and to pensioners. Against these credits to the policy, however, there must be set certain serious debits.

The stream of White Papers from 1944 onwards (chronicled in Chapter Three) developed a view of inflation – the association of inflation with full employment, requiring in the first instance *general* restraint in increases in prices and incomes, a prescription later revealed to be inadequate and giving place to the view that action rather was required on *specific* prices and incomes. By contrast the White Paper setting out the proposals for Stage Two proffers no analysis of inflation. All it does is to record that 'Inflation is a worldwide problem'. From this point of view it is the most barren of the entire array of governmental White Papers stretching back for over a quarter of a century. Not surprisingly therefore it does not provide any reasoning for the figures contained in the proposals, the economic logic and the political fairness of which may on this account be somewhat suspect.

It is not difficult to understand this vacuum. There had come into office in 1970 a Conservative Government with a strong reaction against the 'interventionist' policies of its predecessor. This reaction was based both on the neglect of the need for 'non-partisanship' for the effective exercise of Government, and on the mistaken understanding of the true conservative philosophy that institutions must develop in response to the pressure of events. It was believed instead that a modern society would respond automatically to mechanical regulators such as unemployment and the supply of money. It had thus fallen into the trap which sometimes waylays the conservative-minded – that of championing the ideology of yester-year. When events proved the Government wrong, it did not attempt to build on the foundations already laid by previous experience in the United Kingdom, but it proceeded to borrow from another country – the United States. There, as we saw in Chapter Nine, it is the conventional – though not everybody's – belief that all that is required is a temporary set of measures and a transient apparatus. This book has given reasons why this is a superficial view. But it is this view which would appear to have shaped the agencies.

During Stage Two the agencies are simply to give orders: to restrain wage and price increases and to roll back unwarranted wage and price increases, calling on the Government to enforce their orders if it so happens that they are defied. There is no indication that the agencies will be required to give reasons for such orders, rather the contrary. Yet without reasons how can the agencies carry conviction in the short run and retain support in the long run? More important: how, with summary orders and no reasons, are the agencies to transform themselves into bodies (or a body) which can seek in the first instance to persuade firms and trade unions to observe the rules of price and wage behaviour as suggested in Chapter Twelve? Or how, indeed, immersed in the issue of summary orders, can the agencies think out long-term policies at all? True, there might, for example, be appointed to the Pay Board a Deputy Chairman enjoined specifically to think of the longer term; but the long-term policy must spring from the short-term investigations. It may be added that thinking of the longer term is more important in the sphere of prices than of incomes. Academic specialists in industrial relations have thought a lot about incomes policies, but economists in general have given unfortunately little consideration to price policies. All these are important questions requiring answers; there is no indication that the agencies are designed to develop them.

These then are doubts about the suitability of the proposals for Stage Two for the longer term. It is to be hoped that the doubts will be belied. For there are at least two reasons why the United Kingdom, more than most countries, should need a valid long-term policy. In the first place Britain, more than most other countries, is affected by the pressure of the world's rapidly growing population on resources, for she is a large food importer. One need not believe all the dire forecasts of the ecologists, but the pressure of population on world food supplies may become a real one resulting in rising food prices in the United Kingdom; and food constitutes one quarter of the average British household's budget. Since people are concerned with their real earnings it is important to mitigate the impact of rising food prices on standards of living. Given that British entry to the Common Market is irreversible, the British Government ought to press urgently for a review of the Common Market Agricultural Policy, so as to lessen or reduce the 'price' of maintaining agricultural production; in the meantime it must soften the effects of higher food prices through appropriate social policies, not only increased family allowances but also, if necessary, reductions in rates of income tax. Certainly in the future the Government will have to be far more ready and willing to 'buy' support from the public by making appropriate fiscal concessions to offset the impact on living standards of its own policies and of Common Market policies, whatever these may be.

In the second place we have argued that the wage lead could be set, not only by the leading economic sector in one country, but also by the economically leading country (p. 22). As things now are, the United Kingdom will not be the economically leading country in the European Economic Community; she will be among the followers. Productivity in manufacturing is higher and it is also moving upwards faster in most other countries of the Community than it is in the United Kingdom. There must then follow an upward pull or push on British wages. In seeking to deal with this problem the United Kingdom will be operating in a milieu not generally sympathetic to prices and incomes policies (it was seen in Chapter Nine that the only country in the Community which has given serious attention to the problems of prices and incomes is Holland). The other Community members have for the greater part tried to confine their answers to inflation simply to monetary and fiscal policies.

The projected integration of the European economies means that inflation will now be a joint problem, but, paradoxically, differing rates of inflation among member countries make that integration all the more difficult to attain. These differing rates of inflation will not be overcome through a monetary union only, for we have seen that monetary policies do not in themselves deal with the social and political causes of rising prices and may indeed, pushed beyond a point, aggravate them. It is therefore not only in the interests of the United Kingdom but also vital to the wider European Community that *new* policies to deal with the *new* inflation should be an integral part of the European venture.

29 January 1973

Appendix

Equation 1   : $pQ = wL + rK$

where p = the implied G D P deflator measured as an index with a base value of 1.

                 Q = a unit of real G D P taken at the same base year as p.

                 w = average earnings

                 L = the total number of workers

                 r = the return on a unit of capital at replacement cost

                 K = the total number of units of capital at replacement cost

This equation defines the money value of G D P, that is, pQ, as the sum of all wages, that is, wL, and all profits, that is, rK.

Equation 2   : $p = \dfrac{wL}{Q} + \dfrac{rK}{Q}$

This equation shows that movements in the price of G D P will be a function of changes in total labour costs per unit of real output (wL/Q) assuming that the return on capital and the capital-output ratio (K/Q) are constant.

Equation 3   : $r\dfrac{K}{Q} = p - \dfrac{wL}{Q}$

This equation shows that, if the capital-output ratio (K/Q) is constant, changes in the rate of profit will depend on the relation between changes in prices and changes in unit labour costs.

Equation 4   : $1 = \dfrac{1}{p}\dfrac{wL}{Q} + \dfrac{1}{p}\dfrac{rK}{Q}$

This equation shows that the share of labour in national income, wL/pQ, will be affected positively by changes in unit labour costs, wL/Q, and negatively by changes in the price level, p.

Index